THE NEW CREATION

THE NEW CREATION

Herbert McCabe O.P.

continuum

Continuum International Publishing Group
The Tower Building   80 Maiden Lane
11 York Road   Suite 704
London SE1 7NX   New York, NY 10038

www.continuumbooks.com

First published by Sheed and Ward, 1964.
This edition published by Continuum, 2010.

British Library Cataloguing-in-Publication Data
A catalogue record for this book is available from the British Library.

ISBN: 978-1441-14573-4

Designed and typeset by Newgen Imaging Systems Pvt Ltd, Chennai, India

ACKNOWLEDGEMENT

Author and publisher wish to acknowledge their debt to the editors of *The Life of the Spirit* and *Blackfriars,* in which much of the material of this book made its first appearance.

CONTENTS

TO BERNARD AND LUCY

PREFACE

Herbert McCabe died in 2001. Since his death several posthumous works of his have appeared and all of them have been very well reviewed. Their favorable review is not surprising since McCabe was an extraordinarily gifted thinker and author. He was a great philosopher. But he was also a great theologian. He was very much a disciple of Thomas Aquinas, whose thinking pervades almost all that he wrote. Yet he often used to say that Aquinas was not a Thomist—the point being that Aquinas would have been horrified at the thought of his writings being taken to be the last word on the topics discussed by him. McCabe always sought to treat Aquinas as someone who might be brought into contemporary debates, both philosophical and theological. This is very evident from his posthumously published texts.

But it is also evident from what he published in his lifetime, as the present book clearly shows. *The New Creation* originally appeared in 1964 and is certainly one of McCabe's best works. Written with his characteristic clarity and wit, and containing many of the emphases that marked his later writings, it can be read as his most sustained essay in biblical theology. Its focus is the sacraments of the Church, but, working on the principle that to theologize well depends on understanding the theology of the past, the book ranges copiously over Old and New Testament passages while trying to indicate what sacraments can mean today. People have often told me how impressive and helpful they have found it, so it is very good that Continuum is now reprinting it.

In terms of its insights and sheer readability, *The New Creation* is a truly excellent book. Its theology is superb and very relevant to us as we currently try to think about the nature and significance of sacraments. Readers will discover that, given the date of its first publication, McCabe sometimes refers to liturgical norms that are not now prevalent (he assumes, for example, that Catholic priests regularly celebrate the Eucharist with their backs to the congregation). It is, however, a sign of McCabe's theological genius that such references detract not one whit from the profundity of the thinking that McCabe tries to convey in the book. Good introductions to sacramental theology are hard to come by. *The New Creation* is one not to be missed at all costs.

Brian Davies OP
Fordham University
New York

INTRODUCTION

CHRIST is present to us in so far as we are present to each other. We are born with a constitutional inability to live together in love; we achieve a precarious unity only with great difficulty and for a short time; there is a flaw in the very flesh we have inherited which makes for division between us. The very thing that should make us one, the fact that we come into existence as members of one family, is the source of our isolation. The nature in which we are born is twisted and tends to alienate us from each other. Whatever community we try to set up by purely human means, whether it be the family or the political community, we fail to reach real unity. This is the story of Babel; in the city built by men to reach to the heavens, the tongues of men are confused and they fail to understand one another.

St. Luke's account of Pentecost shows us the way in which human community will be reached; with the coming of the Spirit of Christ, men who have hitherto been divided by language and culture come to understand one another. The teaching of the Bible is that the goal of mankind, real unity in love amongst men, can only be reached by dying to our injured human nature—the unity we have as members of Adam's race—and rising again to a new physical human community in the risen Christ. The human race, astonishingly, is not destined to die out as other species have done, to be replaced by others in the course of evolution. It will be transformed and live eternally. Transformed humanity will not as a whole exist physically until the second coming of Christ; then we shall rise again with our flesh cured of its weakness and glorified by the divine life it will share.

Already, however, because of the resurrection of Christ, the new humanity exists. His risen body is the foundation of the new human race. Already, moreover, we can belong to the new creation, not yet physically but sacramentally; our bodies make contact, real contact, with the risen Christ through mysteries, symbols in which he is present to us. In these same mysteries we are able to be really present to each other. The sacraments can be regarded as mysteries of human community, as symbolizing the union in the Spirit between men which they bring about, as well as mysteries of Christ's action or of his bodily presence. These two ways of looking at them come, indeed, to the same thing.

This book is a study of the sacraments as mysteries of human unity, as the ways in which men are able to break down the barriers between them and form a real community. It is a study, therefore, of the sacraments as constituting the Church, for the Church is nothing but the community which sacramentally foreshadows the life for which God has destined man. She is, so to speak, a living picture of the unity that God has in store for the human race. But she is not just a picture; because Christ is risen her mysteries do not simply show forth something in the future, they also partially realize something that is present. In the Church the new creation is already realized, though in a hidden way. It is because of our realism about the bodily resurrection of Christ that we take a "realist" view of the sacraments. Christ is alive in a human bodily way, and hence he is not just someone to be thought of, to be remembered, to be present only in the mind. These are our ways of trying to reach out to a man who is absent, but Christ is not absent as are the dead, he can be with us in the flesh and his way of being with us is the sacramental system.

We can no longer treat the sacraments, as Catholic writers have sometimes done in the past, as "aids" to the spiritual life which the Church is fortunately able to dispense to her children, we must return to the classical tradition in which they are seen as our living contact with the humanity of Christ through which alone we share in divine life.

The central difficulty of our subject is the notion of "sacramental reality". This is something that crops up whether we begin our discussion with the Church as a whole or with some individual sacrament. In both cases we are dealing with something that eludes our ordinary categories of thought. Thus, the Church is not simply the visible organization of men and institutions in the sense that a political community is a visible organization; nor, on the other hand, is her reality to be found in some quite invisible community—the community of those who actually love God, or the community of the predestined. In the same way, the sacraments are not simply the external gestures that can be seen by anyone, nor is their reality something purely invisible. Both of the Church and of the sacraments we have to say that they exist at some intermediate level, or at least that they cannot exhaustively be described at either level. In a sense the purpose of this book is to draw attention to this intermediate level of reality, for here Church and sacraments are one; the sacraments show themselves as different aspects of the life of the Church; the Church appears as the great sacrament, the mystery of Christ's presence amongst us.

The sacramental reality is an object of faith, hidden from the unbeliever who sees merely the outward sign of it, but it is not the final object of faith. It is itself a symbol leading the believer on to a greater depth of mystery. Faith is a process of penetration into the divine life, it does not find rest in anything short of the Father. Through the sacramental life of the Church we reach to living union with the humanity of Christ but this of its nature carries us on to his divinity, and even the divinity of the Son is no terminus, for his whole being is to be a relation to the Father. Even when faith has matured by death and resurrection into the vision of God we shall not have reached something static, fixed, comprehensible; eternal life is an unceasing exploration of the infinite abyss of the Godhead.

The sacramental life, however, is not concerned with this vision of God, it belongs to the era of faith. The sacraments, indeed, are the expression of faith peculiar to the strange interim period between the resurrection of Christ and our resurrection. The intermediate reality of the sacraments is, indeed, connected with the intermediate character of our era. We live in an age which is neither, like that of the Old Testament, simply prior to the new creation, nor yet fully present to it. The sacraments are the ways in which the last things are partially realized, the intersection of the new world and the world made out of date by the resurrection of Christ. When the old world has finally passed away there will be no place for faith or for the sacraments of faith; organized religion as a special part of life will cease to exist. When man really comes to himself and achieves his goal he will have progressed beyond religion.

There is one striking omission from this book for which I must simply apologize; to deal with it adequately would have doubled the length of the work. I have only dealt in passing and by allusion with the theology of Mary. This should seem a startling omission to any modern Catholic, for in the classical tradition which is being rediscovered in our time (sometimes under the name of the "new" theology) the theology of the Virgin Mother Church is closely interrelated with that of the Virgin Mother of Christ. When they have been separated, as has sometimes happened in the past, both have suffered; devotion to Mary has become sentimental and even superstitious, while the image of the Church has become legalistic and authoritarian. I believe it is extremely significant that the revitalized Church of our day has been characterized both by a new understanding of the Christian community as the body of Christ and by an unprecedented devotion to Mary. A great many Christians both within and outside the Church of Rome are understandably suspicious of this latter phenomenon; to them it looks like just another upsurge of Mariolatry. I would appeal to such people to examine it fairly for what it is and not simply to repeat criticisms which may have been valid in another age; to me it seems something quite new and an essential part of the new life in the Church. In the Virgin Israel, the Virgin Mary, the Bride of the Lamb, we have one of the most fundamental scriptural images of *grace*—the fertility which is not of any human power but simply from God, and in this image we have the great type of the Church. In the Virgin Mary we believe we see fulfilled the life which Christ promises to those he loves; her assumption into the new creation is the type and pledge of our union with his resurrection and our real human life in the world to come.

Readers will not, I hope, be too irritated by a certain amount of repetition and overlapping between different parts of the book (Chapter 9, for example, is an expansion of some remarks made at the end of Chapter 5). Although conceived as a unity, the book was not written at one sitting, but was gradually produced in the form of lectures to a variety of audiences. Most of the chapters have grown out of discussions with students and others at various English universities and at conferences of the Union of Catholic Students. I should like to thank all those who took part in these for their criticisms, arguments and questions which have helped me to clarify the ideas I here put forward. I also especially thank Fr. Laurence Bright, O.P., who read and improved almost all the chapters.

HERBERT MCCABE, O.P.
MARTHA'S VINEYARD
JULY 1963

1

THE WORD OF GOD

THIS book will be about revelation, about the community God has established, and about the sacraments that constitute it; theological, concerned with God and his dealings with men. Most of what I say will probably be pretty familiar stuff, but some of it may be new; this is because I shall be drawing on the results of the great theological revival which has been going on for some years in the Church but which has not yet had its full effect in England. A word in passing about this revival, because we shall be constantly coming back to it. It is one aspect of a quiet reformation, a surge of new life within the Church. The most obvious signs of this are the liturgical movement, the return to the Scriptures and the Fathers and, above all, the new understanding of the place of the laity in the Church. There is a good deal in common between this movement of reform and the reformation which went sour on us in the sixteenth century. Quite a lot of what we shall be saying would have delighted the heart of Martin Luther, for example. Indeed, it is precisely because it would have delighted his heart that it tended to be shelved by Catholics of the Counter-Reformation. The urgent task then was to defend the Church against nationalism and it was more important to stress the differences between Protestants and Catholics than the similarities. Now the situation has changed a good deal and many of the ideas that had been kept in the dark have been brought out into the light, where they are flourishing immensely.

Theology exists because God did not only make man, he also spoke to him. Here when I say, "theology" I mean what is sometimes called "revealed theology", as opposed to natural theology.

There seems to me to be such a great difference between these two that it is a mistake to use the same word for both. What is called "natural theology" is a part of philosophy; it is a certain kind of reflection on the world, it has no immediate connection with faith or dogma. It is true that philosophers, generally speaking, are the most dogmatic of men, but they cannot claim any divine authority for their dogmatism. The kind of philosophical reflection that is called "natural theology" exists because God made the world and men. I think that this reflection can lead to the conclusion that there is a "beyond" that transcends all that we can know. Broadly speaking, we look at the world and it has a created look about it, which is as far as we can go. There used to be an idea (invented, I think, by Pascal) that the God of the philosophers was a different kind of being from the God of Abraham, Isaac, and Jacob. Now of course the God of the philosophers that Pascal had in mind may very well be different from the God of Abraham, Isaac, and Jacob, but the God of my philosophy (and here I am at one with St. Thomas) is not well known enough to be different from Yahweh of the Old Testament. Philosophy tells us almost nothing about God, certainly not enough to set up a rival religion.

God made me and he made the whole world; and this is the reason why it is possible, by reflecting upon the world, to come to know that God exists. This kind of reflection is a matter of philosophy, and like any other important or interesting philosophical question, it is a matter of great controversy. So far as I know, no philosopher has ever held an interesting position which has not been rejected by the majority of other philosophers, and this business of arriving philosophically at the existence of God is no exception to the rule. Like all other philosophical positions, it is a minority opinion. However, so far as I am concerned this does not matter, since the minority includes myself. I want to stress that this is a philosophical opinion but I mention it here because this kind of philosophical reflection is also called theology—"natural theology". I am not, in this book, going to be concerned directly with "theology" in that sense. Natural theology is possible, in my view, because God made me; theology in the strict sense, in the sense in which I am using it, is possible because God has not only made me but has spoken to me. Theology, in fact, begins not just with the action of God but with the word of God.

The central teaching of our religion is that we are not merely creatures of God. Besides creating us as the highest kind of material creature, God has called us to share in his own uncreated life. This share in the life of God himself is what we call grace. It is extremely important to realize that a creature with grace is not just a higher kind of creature—in the sense, for example, that a creature with intelligence is a higher kind of creature than one without. Grace does not make man a better kind of creature, it raises him beyond creaturehood, it makes him share in divinity. This share in divinity is first of all expressed by the fact that we are not merely things created, we are creatures who are on speaking terms with God. Because of the divine life in us, the Spirit of God in us, we are able to listen to what God says—this is what we call faith. Because of the divine life in us we are able to speak back to God. As St. Paul says: "The Spirit comes to the rescue of our weakness; for we do not know what to ask for in order to pray properly, but the Spirit himself prays for us." (Rom. 8.26.)

Now what exactly do we mean by "the Word of God"? The question is not all that easy to answer; in fact the whole of this chapter will be spent in failing to answer it. It is one of the characteristics of the key phrases in religious discussion that their meaning cannot be exhausted by a simple definition— the same, of course, is true of important philosophical terms. Whereas in, say, physics, the vast majority of technical terms have a simple and adequate definition, this is not the case in theology. I think there are good reasons for this but I shall not go into them now; roughly, I should say that it comes about because theology, like philosophy, is very largely concerned with what is specifically human, and human nature in the end transcends the limits of human language. Our language is at home with objects; it has difficulty with subjects. When I say that the key theological terms cannot be simply defined I do not mean that they are inexact or woolly. The difficulty with them is that they have application at many different levels, and an explanation which will do at one level is inadequate at another. In this respect there is a certain resemblance between theological language and the language of poetry, you can go on seeing more and more depth of meaning in a poetic image without ever exhausting its implications, and the same is true of a statement such as: "The Word was made flesh and dwelt among us."

Of course it can happen, and it has happened, that theologians forget the depth of meaning in their words. This accounts for the dreary and futile business that you often get in manuals of theology; a matter of solving verbal puzzles instead of dealing with human and divine mysteries. Our most respectable Catholic newspaper has a column in which a theologian answers readers' queries. It is, alas, headed: "Here's the answer." I suppose this is inevitable in journalism, but it is a pity that the impression is given that theological questions can be answered in a kind of pious quiz. In theology as in philosophy there are no slick answers, which is perhaps why theologians and philosophers talk so interminably.

One reason why theological terms behave like poetic images is that the language which God chose for speaking to us is very often the language of poetry. God did not provide us with a divinely inspired manual of doctrine; instead he gave us a library of all kinds of books, a great number of which are books of poetry. The Bible is the first thing we mean when we speak of the Word of God. Later we shall look into the Bible to see what it says about itself, to see what the word of God says about the word of God, but first I want to say something in general about the theological purpose of the Bible.

St. Thomas remarked that whereas men can talk only with words and gestures, God can talk with the course of history itself. He can guide the course of events in such a way as to give them a significance which reveals him to us. This is what he has done with his chosen people; he has so ordered their history that the events themselves tell us of him. The history of the Hebrews not only leads up to the revelation of God in Christ, it also foreshadows it. The development of the Hebrew people already tells us about Christ, and in fact Christ is unintelligible without this background. The history of the Hebrews is like a play; things happen in the first act which symbolize themes in the play but the symbolism is only fully appreciated when we get to Act Five. It is not just the words of the play, but the action, which carries the meaning. Frequently in a play the characters do not themselves recognize the full meaning or symbolic character of what they do and say, hence what we used to call "dramatic irony". The same is true of the sacred drama of Hebrew history. Normally the Hebrews did not get beyond recognizing that their history did have a divine significance. They realized that they had a definite destiny preordained by God, that they were fulfilling a divine plan, but the shape of this destiny was hidden from them. Some of them, however, were given a greater insight into the divine plan, and these are the men we call prophets. The special character of the prophet is not precisely that he predicts the future, but that he sees the working of the divine plan in the life of his people, he predicts the future just in so far as this plan points forward to the future.

God, however, has not merely given us a divine history; he has also given us an authentic interpretation of that history. This is the Bible. The one thing that all the books of the Bible have in common is that they all have something to do with the

Chosen People and their destiny, but they do not simply chronicle events; the history is written up in such a way as to highlight its significance for the divine plan. The books of Samuel, for example, do for the history of Saul and David much the same thing as Shakespeare does for, say Julius Caesar: what we have is more than a record of facts, it is an interpreted record. The difference is that here we have a uniquely authentic interpretation because the author of the interpretation is also the author of the facts themselves.

In sacred history, then, we have first of all persons, things and events which have a significance of their own, and then their significance is brought out and made clear through the words of Scripture which describe them. As we shall see, in this the Bible resembles the sacraments. In each of the sacraments there is first of all a symbolic significant gesture or thing, which we call the "matter" of the sacrament, and then the significance of this is brought out and made clear by words, which we call the "form". The sacraments, like the Bible, are revelations of God, and their structure, so to speak, is the same. But more of this later.

The Hebrew people had a history—this is the most important thing about them—but the Bible too has a history. It was not written all at one time; it is, as I said, a library of books, some of them centuries older than others. In the Bible we can watch the gradual process by which the Hebrews became more and more aware of the significance of their destiny. We can watch the growth of certain key ideas, certain words and images which slowly acquire a traditional symbolism. The imagery of a language embodies the life of the people who use it, and the richness and complexity of the religious language of the Chosen People result from their divinely guided history. The meanings of their words are full of historical associations. To understand, for example, what an image like the "Shepherd" meant for them, it is necessary to know about the history of Abel and Abraham and Moses and David and so on. Poetic imagery is used by certain writers and then handed down enriched to be used by later ones. In fact it is possible to think of the whole Old Testament history as a period during which God was slowly preparing and maturing a language which would be fit for use in speaking of his Son. Let us watch this process at work in the case of the image of the Word of God. St. John says simply, "In the beginning was the Word . . . and the Word was made flesh and pitched his tent among us." Let us unpack some of the meaning contained in this phrase.

"The Lord Yahweh", said one of the early prophets, "does nothing without revealing his secret to his servants the prophets. The lion has roared: who will not fear? The Lord Yahweh has spoken; who can but prophesy?" (Amos 3.7–8.)

This passage sums up the thought of the Hebrews in the eighth century before Christ about the connection between the action of God and his revelation of himself. The acts of God are all revelations of his "secret", his mysterious plan, and at every stage in the plan God reveals the significance of his acts to the Prophets. God acts and speaks simultaneously. As a matter of fact the Hebrew language has a word, *dabar,* which means both word and deed. The word of God always accomplishes something. This is seen most clearly in the fifth-century poem about creation which begins Genesis:

God said, "Let there be light", and there was light . . .

God said, "Let there be a firmament in the midst of the waters" . . . etc.

God said, "Let us make man in our own image, after our likeness . . ."

At each stage in this vision of creation, God speaks and his word is creative. This was not, of course, a bright original idea of the author of this creation poem. He is drawing here upon an imagery which had become traditional, almost a cliche, in Hebrew literature. There are plenty of other examples of it scattered throughout the Old Testament:

> By the Word of Yahweh the heavens were made and all their
> host by the breath of his mouth.
>
> [Ps. 33.]

> Lift up your eyes and see
> who created these
> He brings out their host by number
> calling them all by name. [Isa. 40.26.]

> Let all thy creatures serve thee
> for thou hast spoken and they were made
> thou didst send forth thy breath and they were created and
> nothing can resist thy voice. [Judith 16.17.]

The Word of God is then first of all creative, or to put it the other way round, creation is word from God. His acts tell us of him.

> The heavens tell of the glory of Yahweh
> and the firmament proclaims his handiwork
> . . . their voice is not heard
> yet their voice goes through all the earth
> and their words to the end of the world. [Ps. 19.]

But it was not first of all as creator of the whole world that the Hebrews saw God as revealing himself. First of all he revealed his secret plan in the way he guided their history. The Word of God is first of all heard in the creation and government of the Hebrews; it is only later that this is extended to the world as a whole.

The turning-point of history for the Hebrews was the Exodus, for this was the moment when they were created as a people. This great deed is always in their minds when they think of Yahweh. He is "Your God who brought you out of the land of Egypt". This is what they celebrate every year in the Passover. At this feast they remember each year who they are; they are the people created by God, brought out from Egypt to accomplish a mysterious divine destiny. In its primitive origins the Pasch was almost certainly a feast of the seasons, a feast of new life, just as the Christian pasch of Easter is bound up with the pagan spring festivals of the dying god and new life—but more of this later on. The important point is that the Hebrews used the feast of new life to celebrate the new life of Israel. Israel had gone down into a kind of death in Egypt, just as the dying god of Middle-Eastern religions goes down into the underworld each year. Now at the Pasch Israel rose from the dead, came up from the grave and passed through the waters of the Red Sea to be welded into a new people. All these ideas, which we shall see being developed in the theology of the Resurrection and Christian baptism, are already present in the thought of the prophets of Israel.

The great deeds of the Exodus are accomplished by the word of God. Just as the stars of heaven are called into being by this word—

He brings out their host by number
calling them all by name. [Isa. 40.26.]

—so Israel is called out of Egypt by the word of God:

When Israel was a child I loved him
and out of Egypt I called my son,

says Hosea, and goes on:

The more I called them, the more they went from me.
[Hos. 11.1–2.]

It is the word of God which slays the Egyptians, according to the author of the Book of Wisdom:

While deep silence covered all things
and night was in the midst of her course

from the heights of heaven, thy almighty word
leapt down from the royal throne
a fierce warrior into the midst of a land
devoted to destruction. [Wisd. of Sol. 18.14–15.]

As you read these passages I expect you will be reminded
of their application in the New Testament to the Word made
flesh. In fact St. Matthew, who constantly wants to make the
point that Christ himself is the new Israel, refers back to the
passage from Hosea when he tells the story of the flight into
Egypt. "Out of Egypt I have called my son." And the passage
about the Word leaping down from his royal throne during the
silence of the night is used in one of the masses of Christmas-
tide to refer to the birth of Christ.

The word of God not only creates the People of God but it
also comes to them in the form of the Law. God speaks to
Moses on Mount Sinai and in so far as Israel receives this
word of God and keeps the Law, she remains a distinctive
people, a special community. The presence of the Law, the
presence of the word of God, preserves the identity of the
Hebrews. Whenever they turn from the Law they tend to min-
gle with the surrounding nations and this compromises their
distinctive identity as it compromises their destiny.

The Book of Exodus, after giving the story of the delivery
of Israel from Egypt (or rather, after giving at least two rather
different stories of the delivery from Egypt), goes on to speak
of the giving of the Law, the Ten Commandments. Then there
are many strange pages about how to make something called
the Ark of the Covenant and the great tent or tabernacle. The
point of the Ark is that it was the dwelling-place of the Word
of God:

In the ark you shall put the testimony that I shall give you.
There I will meet with you, and from above the mercy seat

. . . I will speak with you of all that I will give you in commandment for the people of Israel. [Exod. 25.21–2.]

The Ark dwells in the great tent, and it is ceremonially installed there, at a significant date:

> Yahweh said to Moses: On the first day of the first month, you shall erect the tabernacle of the tent of meeting. And you shall put in it the ark of the testament. [Exod. 40.1]

The meaning of this ceremony is that the word of God, dwelling in the Ark, has pitched his tent among the people of Israel. And this, of course, is what St. John is referring back to when he says "The Word became flesh and pitched his tent among us" (the phrase "dwelt amongst us" is an impoverishment of St. John's words).

The word of God is thus for the Hebrews not merely something that is listened to and understood, it is creative and lifegiving. The Hebrew people were created by the word of God and the Word dwells among them to give them life. In a famous passage in the Book of Deuteronomy, Yahweh is represented as saying that he allowed Israel to go hungry in the desert for forty years but fed them with manna, with "bread from heaven", so that "he might make you know that man does not live by bread alone but by everything that comes forth from the mouth of God". (Deut. 8.3.) Here the word of God is compared to the bread by which a man lives. The bread of Israel is to be the word of God. This, needless to say, is the background to the eucharistic theology of St. John.

There is no need here for more detailed investigation into the Old Testament development of the image of the word of God; the essential point is that the word of God does not merely convey information, it is creative of the People of God, it is creative in fact of the whole world, it dwells among the People of God to preserve them, it is their bread which brings them life.

The word of God is his presence in the world both revealing him and giving life to the world. The thing is summed up in a famous poem in the Book of Isaiah:

As the rain and snow come down from heaven and return
   not thither until they have watered the earth
making it bring forth and sprout,
giving seed to the sower and bread to the eater, so shall my
   word be that goes forth from my mouth;
it shall not return to me empty,
but it shall accomplish that which I purpose and prosper in
   the thing for which I sent it. [Isa. 55.10–11.]

This is the picture upon which St. John bases the structure of the poem with which he begins his gospel. The picture is of the Word of God coming out from God, bringing fertility and life to the world, and then returning once more to God having accomplished his purpose. The prologue begins with the Word "with God", it comes to its climax when the "Word was made flesh and pitched his tent among us" and then finishes with the Word once more "in the bosom of the Father". It has recently been suggested that there is, in fact, an exact correspondence between the verses on the way down and the way up.

The point I want to stress is that when St. John came to write he had ready formed for him the image of the word of God. You might say that the New Testament comes about by taking the Old Testament literally. What in the Old Testament was a metaphorical way of describing the action of God in the world becomes in the New Testament a literal account. The thing is that unless we realize that the literal account is the concrete realization of an image, we miss the meaning. In the New Testament the pictures have come to life, but the fact that they are alive must not make us forget that they are pictures. To take a look forward into a later chapter in the Eucharist our bread really and literally is the Word of God, but we only see the point of it when we remember the metaphor of which this is the concrete realization.

In the notion of the word of God, the ideas of knowledge and life are tied up together. The Word shows us God and at the same time brings us life from him, in fact brings us his life. This is why St. John fixed on this image to describe Christ; by receiving Christ we receive together knowledge of God and the life of God. We are given new life, reborn as new creatures, by coming to know God. The constant intertwining of the words "light" and "life" in St. John's Gospel teach us the same thing:

> What came to be in him was life
> and life was the light of mankind. [John 1.4.]

We can say either that this gospel is about the conquest of darkness by light, or the victory of life over death.

The response to the word of God is faith, and faith involves life:

> He that believes in the Son has everlasting life. He that does not believe shall not see life. [John 3.36.]

> He that believes in me has everlasting life. I am the bread of life. [John 6.47–8.]

> I am resurrection, I am life.
> He that believes in me, even though he be dead, shall live.
> Everyone that lives and believes in me shall not die for ever. [John 11.25.]

and so on; there are dozens of places where this kind of thing is said in St. John's Gospel. Receiving the word of God is not just a matter of getting to know something, it is a matter of receiving a more intense life, the life of God himself.

These two aspects of the word of God are very clearly brought out in the structure of the Mass. This begins with a liturgy of the word of God in which the emphasis is on the knowledge side—the reading of the word in the Epistle and Gospel. It is followed by the sacrifice in which the emphasis is on the Word of God as life-giving; he is present to the sacramental symbols of food and drink.

There is no doubt at all that in the past few centuries we have tended to let these two fall far apart. Catholics, especially since the Reformation, have played down both the life-giving character of the Scriptures and the symbolic character of the Eucharist. Some Protestants had denied the real presence of Christ's body and blood in the Eucharist and said that the bread and wine were *merely* symbolic. This naturally led them to lay a much emphasis did than contemporary Catholics did on the presence of God in the Scriptures. Catholics, nervous of Protestant contagion—and perhaps especially nervous of being mistaken for Protestants by the Inquisition—leaned over backwards to say the opposite. The actual Scriptures ceased to be thought of as a nourishment for Catholics, and they substituted books of Christian doctrine. It did not seem to them scandalous or even particularly surprising that the Epistle and Gospel at Mass should be read in an inaudible murmur in a foreign language by someone standing with his back to them—it is all right because soon he will turn round and tell us quite audibly about the catechism and the second collection.

In the same way it was equally forgotten that the Eucharist is symbolic, that it shows us something, is a revelation of God. But more of this in a later article.

There can be no doubt, then, that for St. John and the early Church, the response to Christ which they call faith, the reception of the Word of God, is something that brings life with it. Of course we must not think of the response to faith as something which comes from our side to meet the Word of God coming from God's side. The response to the Word is a part of the coming of the Word, it is the Word in us.

"No man can come to me unless the Father who sent me draws him." [John 6.44.] Both revelation and faith come from the Father. He sends his Word to us and draws us to his Word.

This notion of faith as a living response to Christ is the principal meaning of the word in the New Testament, whether in St. John or St. Paul, and it is one which the Protestant Churches have on the whole stressed very strongly. When a Protestant says we are saved by faith alone, it is normally faith in this sense that he has in mind, faith in the sense of complete abandonment to Christ, a turning from reliance on created things to reliance solely upon the Word of God. This is, as I say, the primary sense of the word "faith", but there is another sense in which, for example, St. Paul distinguishes it from love and from trust in the fulfilment of God's plan, or hope. When, he says, God's plan has finally come to complete fulfilment, faith and hope will pass away, only love will remain.

In this sense faith refers to a particular aspect of our response to Christ, our reliance on the Word of God for insight into God's plan. In this aspect our abandonment to Christ means that we do not rely on our own intellectual powers, but, confronted by God's plan, we (literally) take his Word for it. This is the aspect of faith which is expressed in our assent to truths about God's plan; it is expressed in our proclamation of the Creed.

Faith in this sense is an aspect or part of faith in the full sense, but it is a particularly interesting one because it can be detached and exist by itself without the rest. In other words we can accept, by faith, all that God has taught us, without having the rest of the divine life in us. This is traditionally called "dead faith", faith divorced from its life which is love. It is most important to see that such faith is deformed. Love is not added on to faith from outside; normally faith and love are one thing. Faith without love is something monstrous and incomplete in itself. Certainly this deformed faith is not what St. Paul is speaking of when he says repeatedly that we are saved by faith, nor, when he contrasts faith with works is he contrasting faith with the deeds of love which are a part of true faith. He is contrasting it with works done without faith, which are not of course works of love, for while we can have divine faith without love, we cannot have divine love without faith.

> God who at various times and in different ways spoke to our fathers through the prophets, now in these days, which are the last days, has spoken to us through his Son. [Heb. 1.1–2.]

This is how the Epistle to the Hebrews sums up the biblical idea of God's speech. God speaks first of all in the Scriptures but finally in the person of Christ. And faith is our response to this Word.

I have said that we have theology because God has spoken to us and I have tried to show that this speech is not simply a matter of giving information. The word of God which is the foundation of theology is also lifegiving: it is the source of the life of a community. The source of theology is the source of the Church itself. Theology is an aspect of the life of the Church and we should never try to separate it from the rest of the life of the Church. Nevertheless, as almost any priest working in a parish today will tell you, that is what has happened to a great extent in the past. Theology has come to be thought of as a highly abstract and abstruse subject with no immediate relation to things like hearing confessions or preaching or visiting one's parishioners. Theology is something one does in a seminary and then forgets when one gets down to the practical business of the last sacraments and housey-housey. But all that is at last changing; we are returning at last to the great tradition in which theology is the intellectual aspect of our total response to the word of God. We are returning to a theology

which is immediately related to the Scriptures and also immediately related to our personal Christian lives, a theology which
makes sense of our lives as adult Christians in the world in
which we live.

2

THE PEOPLE OF GOD

IN the previous chapter I showed that the first effect of the Word was to create a community, and this time I want to speak about this community, showing first what it meant for the Old Testament, and then how the notion was deepened in the New. Textbooks sometimes approach this matter by asking themselves whether Christ founded a Church to exist after him, and showing that he did so by reference to various Gospel texts. The inadequacy of this lies in the fact that it conceives the possibility of Christ's not having founded a Church. When we see Christ in the context of Scripture we see that the Church is not an institution which Christ decided to have but might have decided not to have. When we see Christ in this Old-Testament background, as he is presented by the New Testament, we see the Church as inevitable. Of course, God might not have planned to have a Church but this would have meant having a totally different plan for the world. The Father's plan, as we learn from the tremendous last epistles of St. Paul, was to bring all things to fulfilment in Christ. This process by which the world grows to maturity in Christ *is* the Church. The Church, as we shall see, is not a thing, it is a process in time.

I shall choose three main themes from the Old Testament, Israel as chosen people, as sacred people, and as bride of Yahweh. The first is summed up in a text of Deuteronomy:

> You are a people holy to Yahweh: Yahweh your God has chosen you to be a people for his own possession, out of all the peoples that are on the face of the earth. It was not because you were more in number than any other people

that Yahweh set his love upon you and chose you, for you were the fewest of all peoples; but it is because Yahweh loves you and is keeping the oath which he swore to your fathers, that Yahweh has brought you out with a mighty hand, and redeemed you from the house of slavery, from the hand of Pharaoh, king of Egypt. [Deut. 7.6–8.]

Notice first of all the difference between a title like "the Chosen People" and one like "master race" or "ruling class" or "top people". These all involve a claim to be especially suited to some outstanding position. If you are an Aryan you are suited by nature to governing the non-Aryans, and so on. Now, the point of the phrase "Chosen People" is exactly the opposite of this. The Hebrews did not think that their special preeminence came from any special fitness of their own; they thought it came purely from the fact that God had chosen them. Every Hebrew knew that God's purpose was to subdue the world to his rule. He had chosen Israel for this purpose, but not because she was powerful and numerous or in any way suited to the task: ". . . for you are the fewest of all peoples; but it is because Yahweh loves you and is keeping the oath that he swore to your fathers, that Yahweh has brought you out with a mighty hand, and redeemed you from the house of slavery." The Hebrews did not think of themselves as a group of men who had come together and found God. They were a group who had been found by God. Israel is not the result of any human effort, it is purely the gratuitous creation of God. Significantly, the passage I quoted cannot get very far without referring once more to the Exodus, the moment of Israel's creation, and the stories of the Exodus emphasize all the time that it was a work of Yahweh, not of Moses or of the Hebrew people. Indeed, Yahweh brings them out of Egypt in spite of their opposition. Even Moses is occasionally disheartened, while the rest of the people say quite frankly that what they want is a bit of peace and quiet.

Very closely tied up with the idea of being a *chosen* people is the idea of being children of God. At the Exodus Yahweh says to Moses:

> You shall say to Pharaoh: Thus says Yahweh, Israel is my first-born son. And I say to you, let my son go that he may serve me; if you refuse to let him go, behold, I will slay your firstborn son. [Exod. 4.22–3.]

This title of "Son of God" is frequently applied to Israel, especially in the Book of Deuteronomy:

> You are the sons of Yahweh your God . . . You are a people holy to Yahweh your God, and Yahweh has chosen you to be a people for his own possession. [Deut. 14.1.2.]

> Do you thus repay Yahweh, you foolish and senseless people? Is he not your father who created you? [Deut. 32.6.]

Like many of the ancient titles of Israel as a whole, this title is later especially applied to the Messiah king who is to come:

> I shall be his father and he shall be my son. [2 Sam. 7.14.]

This is another case in which we see how the New Testament has taken a phrase from the Old and deepened its meaning.

The second thing the Hebrews said about themselves was that they were a sacred people, a consecrated people, or as they sometimes put it, a holy people:

> You shall be a people holy to Yahweh your God. Yahweh will set you high above all nations that he has made, in praise and in fame and in honour, and you shall be a people holy to Yahweh your God, as he has spoken. [Deut. 26.18–19.]

It would be a great mistake to think that holiness here means first of all moral goodness. Holiness for the Hebrews is the first characteristic of God. What is holy is first of all terrifying, dangerous; God is dangerous not first of all because of his wrath, but because his holiness is of itself destructive of what

is profane. No man can see God and live. He is a fire which
burns up anything that comes within range. When he visits
the earth he is accompanied by all the elemental forces of
destruction:

> The voice of Yahweh is upon the waters
> the God of glory thunders . . .
> the voice of Yahweh breaks the cedars
> Yahweh breaks the cedars of Lebanon . . .
> The voice of Yahweh flashes forth flames of fire
> the voice of Yahweh shakes the wilderness . . .
> The voice of Yahweh makes the oak trees whirl
> and strips the forest bare
> and in his temple all cry "Glory".
> Yahweh sits enthroned above the flood
> Yahweh sits enthroned as king for ever. [Ps. 29.]

The holiness of Israel is a sharing in the holiness of God. This
means that on the one hand she is protected from the destructive power of Yahweh, while the other nations are destroyed;
and on the other hand, she herself is dangerous. It is because
they are dangerous that holy things are set apart; it is not safe
for ordinary people to handle them or come too near them.
This idea that certain things are sacred, as opposed to the
profane world, is, according to Mircea Eliade, the one thing
that all definitions of religious phenomena have in common.
He says:

> It is dangerous to come near any defiled or consecrated
> object in a profane state—without, that is, proper ritual
> preparation. What is called taboo—from a Polynesian word
> that the ethnologists have taken over—means just that: it
> is the fact of things or places or persons being cut off, or
> "forbidden", because contact with them is dangerous.[1]

---

[1] *Patterns in Comparative Religion,* London, Sheed and Ward
(1958), p. 15.

For the Hebrews the whole people is dangerous in this way, set apart from secular nations about her. But on the other hand this means that Israel is herself able to endure the presence of God. Just as the priest is the only man who can safely handle the instruments of sacrifice, because he has been consecrated and belongs himself to the realm of the sacred, so Israel can safely approach God because she is consecrated:

[Yahweh says to her:] "You shall be my possession among all peoples, for all the earth is mine, and you shall be to me a kingdom of priests and a holy nation." [Exod. 19.5–6.]

So Israel is chosen out gratuitously from among the peoples and made the children of God, she is chosen out to be the priestly nation, the representative of mankind who can safely converse with God, can offer him acceptable sacrifice. Israel is the chosen one, the son of God, the priest.

She is priestly because she belongs to the world of the divine, she shares in God's world, she lives by his life. Israel lives by the spirit or breath of God; this is why she can survive the terrifying presence of God. There is no space here to enter fully into this notion of the spirit of God, but there is one detail that is worth noticing. The presence of the spirit of Yahweh was associated by the Hebrews with the ceremony of anointing with oil; the Hebrews were thus an anointed people. This is the origin of the word "Messiah" or, in Greek, "Christ". Israel is the Christ of God.

When they were few in number
. . . wandering from nation to nation . . .
he allowed no one to oppress them,
he rebuked kings on their account,
saying "Touch not my Christ,
do my prophets no harm." [Ps. 104.]

This word "Christ" or "Messiah" is another that was transferred first to the king of Israel as personifying the whole people, then to the king of the future, the Christ who was to come to bring the Spirit of God, the life of God to the whole world.

"Chosen one", "Son of God", "Priest", "Christ"; this is how Israel saw herself. There is one further image that we must look at before we turn to what became of these ideas in the New Testament; this is the image of Israel as the bride of Yahweh. That belongs to the same complex of ideas as those we have seen, because Israel is the *virgin* bride of Yahweh. This theme is first developed in the stories of the barren woman who by the power of God gives birth to a son. There are several such stories in the early part of the Old Testament and their point is always the same. The child who is born is the gift of God; the fertility of the woman is something that owes nothing to man, nothing to natural means, but is purely God-given fertility. The first of these women is Sarah the wife of Abraham, the mother of all the Chosen People. In the Prophets the idea is taken up and developed and applied to the whole people of Israel. The whole people is a virgin set aside for marriage with Yahweh. The phrase "virgin Israel" is very common, especially in Hosea, Jeremiah, Isaiah and Ezekiel. The Exodus is seen as the espousals of the virgin and Yahweh, when Yahweh fell in love with Israel and chose her for his bride. Israel's frequent unfaithfulness to Yahweh is described in terms of unfaithfulness to her lover, as fornication and adultery. The future destiny of Israel is seen as the marriage of the virgin with Yahweh. Sometimes the Messiah is seen as the bridegroom, sometimes as the fruit of the union between Yahweh and the virgin Israel.

I said in my previous chapter that the New Testament comes about by taking the Old Testament literally; what is an image or metaphor in the Old Testament is realized in actual fact in the New. In the New Testament the pictures come to life. And of course the first image to be concretely realized is that of the virgin mother Israel. In the thought of the Prophets it was the destiny of Israel to bring forth salvation not by human means

but by the sheer power of God. It is the love of God for Israel
that is to give her the fertility by which she will bring new life
to the world. This vision is concretely realised in Mary the
virgin mother of Christ. In Mary, the virgin motherhood of
Israel is summed up and represented, in her the marriage
between Yahweh and his bride is first consummated:

> The Holy Spirit shall come upon thee and the power of the
> Most High shall overshadow thee. Therefore the Holy One
> that shall be born of thee shall be called the Son of God.
> [Luke 1.35.]

The Holy One that is born of this union is not only called Son
of God but also all the other titles which began as titles of the
Chosen People. He is also the Chosen One, the Christ, the
consecrated one, the priest of Yahweh. In him all that Israel
under the old law has been doing symbolically, figuratively, in
metaphor, becomes real.

It may seem very strange to say that Jesus, who is after all
one individual man, should be the new Israel; how could a
single man be the People of God? And yet this is the teaching
of the Gospels when we see them in their true context of the
whole Bible. In St. Matthew and St. Luke's Gospels Christ
begins his public life by re-enacting in his personal life the
incidents of the Exodus. He comes up after his baptism from
the Jordan into the desert and here he has three trials, three
conflicts with Satan, each of which corresponds to an incident
in the story of Israel in the desert after she has come up from
the Red Sea. Each of them is a trial or temptation in which
Israel failed and in which Christ succeeds. The Gospels are
full of such parallels, but of course the most important of all
is the culminating scene of the passion, death and resurrection
of Christ which takes place significantly in the context of the
Pasch, so that the passing-over of Christ from life through
death to new life corresponds to the passing of the Hebrews
through the death of Egypt into new life.

The reason why the destiny of the Hebrew people is fulfilled in one individual man is that this individual man is to be
the source of a new People of God. Christ did not just found
a Church as a man might found an organization; he *is* the unity
of the Church. The Church, the new People of God, consists
of those who are in him. There is one life in the Church and
it is the life of Christ. This is the meaning of Pentecost. After
his ascension into heaven Christ poured out his risen life, his
Spirit, into the world so that we could live by it. The Church
is all those who live by the risen life of Christ, which is the
Spirit of Christ, a divine person, the Holy Spirit. The unity of
the Church is not just the unity of a society with common
aims, like a university; it is not just the unity of a society with
a single recognized ultimate authority, like a state; it is not just
the unity of people who think in the same way, like a political
party; it involves something like all these things, but the unity
of the Church is first of all the unity of one *life*. What binds
us together is that we live by the same life, the life of Christ.

This is why the images and words which were originally
coined for use about a whole community and which found a
concrete literal realization in a single man, can now be extended
once again to a whole community. What was said metaphorically about the People of Israel was said literally about Christ,
and now it is said about the new People of Israel, the Church,
those who live in Christ. How is it said about the Church? The
things that are said *metaphorically* of Israel and *literally* of
Christ are said *sacramentally* of the Church.

The history of the Hebrews was, of course, a series of
real events which literally happened, but when we ask about
their theological significance, when we want to interpret their
history as the Bible interprets it, we see its significance as
figurative, as metaphorical, as symbolic of what was to come.
Similarly with the cult of the Hebrews; their sacrifices and
religious ceremonies, the Pasch for example, had no value in
themselves except as foreshadowing the sacrifice of Christ.

When we come to Christ himself we find that the value of his acts lies precisely in the acts themselves, in the fact that they historically occurred. With the theology of the Old Testament we are in the world of metaphor and symbol, with the theology of the Gospels we are in the world of physical fact, with the theology of the Church we are in the world of sacraments. It is because of a *metaphor* that the Hebrews were the Christ, the anointed who lived by the breath of God, the Spirit of God. It is because of the *literal* truth that Jesus of Nazareth lives by the Spirit of God and has done so from all eternity. It is because of the *sacraments* that the Church lives by the Spirit of God. Israel was *metaphorically* the virgin mother who brings salvation into the world, Mary was *literally* the virgin mother who gave birth to Christ, the Church is *sacramentally* the virgin mother who brings Christ into the world. The sacrifice of the paschal lamb was a picture or figure of the world's delivery from sin and union with God, the Crucifixion was in physical fact the sacrifice of the atonement, the Mass is the sacrament of this sacrifice.

I could go on indefinitely multiplying examples of this triad, metaphor, natural reality, sacramental reality, for nothing is more important for understanding the Church than to realize the distinction between sacraments and metaphor or picture on the one hand, and natural reality on the other. Nothing is more important and few things are more difficult. Very briefly the whole of sacramental theology can be summed up in saying that a sacrament is a symbol which makes real what it symbolizes. A sacrament has in common with a metaphor or image, that it symbolizes something, and has in common with the natural world that it involves a reality; but a sacrament is neither of these, nor is it a mixture of both. In the Eucharist, for example, we do not have the body of Christ present in the natural way in which it was present on earth together with a symbolic appearance of bread. This is not what "real presence" implies. On the contrary, in the Eucharist we have the body of Christ present just precisely in so far as it is symbolized by the appearance of bread, but it is *sacramentally* symbolized and therefore made real.

The sacraments, as I suggested in the earlier chapter, are revelations of God, but not everything which shows us God can be called sacramental in the sense in which I am using the term. Of course "sacrament" is one of those key terms of religion which can be interpreted at several different levels, but in its deepest sense it means not just any symbol of God but a symbol which reveals the achievement of God's plan for human destiny. Many people have seen the world of nature as revealing the sacred; "the heavens show forth the glory of Yahweh", and sometimes this is called having a sacramental view of the world. But the sacraments in our deeper sense are signs of the revelation which God has made of himself, signs of the Word of God in history. They are concerned not just with God's creation but with his special plan for humanity. This they have in common with the Scriptures, and just as the Scriptures had to be written by God, so the sacraments had to be instituted by God. We can speak, and the Fathers of the Church constantly did speak, of the sacraments of the old law: that is, the signs, especially the cultic signs, which symbolized the workings of God's plan in the Old Testament. The difference between these signs and the sacraments of the new law is just that God's plan has now been realized in Christ. The sacraments of the new law are not simply looking forward to something which is not yet, they symbolize something actually present.

It would be a mistake, however, to think of the symbolism of the sacraments as confined to the present. This mistake is encouraged by the catechism definition of a sacrament as an "outward sign of inward grace". A sacrament is this, but its symbolism is much wider than this suggests. Sacramental symbolism, according to St. Thomas, always embraces the whole history of God's plan, past, present and future. The symbolism of each sacrament looks backward to its institution by Christ and through this to the Old-Testament preparation; it looks to the present effect in the soul and it looks forward to the completion of God's plan in the second coming of Christ.

This last point is important. The earliest Christians, especially those who lived at Thessalonica, expected Christ to return from heaven to earth at any moment. They were disappointed at the delay. In fact, the earliest letters we have by St. Paul were written to reassure them, in particular to assure them that even if they died before Christ came back they would still have eternal life. Nowadays Christians seem to have gone to the opposite extreme, and have practically forgotten about the return of Christ. When a modern Christian thinks of the last day, which is not often, it is almost entirely in terms of the Last Judgement; will he scrape through or not, like an exam. It is not something he looks forward to with passionate longing. Every Sunday in the Creed he says that he waits for, or looks forward to, the resurrection of the dead and life everlasting, but there is not much sign of this in his usual thinking. The last day is, of course, the day of crisis, the day of judgement, but it is also the day of resurrection and life, the day of the coming of Jesus in triumph, when Christ the King is revealed as such. The exclusive concentration on the judgement side of things comes to us partly from the medieval obsession with sin, but partly also from forgetting that our religion is an interpretation of history. Christianity is about the history of mankind, but we too often think of it as good advice instead of good news. This is one of the reasons why Marxism makes an appeal. It contains an authoritative teaching about the course of history, which fills a gap left by our inadequate preaching of Christianity. People want to know about the destiny of mankind, want to know whether history has a meaning, and what it is. Christianity does in fact give an answer here. Just as the Marxist looks forward to the millennium and the final withering-away of the State, so the Catholic looks forward impatiently to the withering-away of the organized Church. For the whole set-up of faith, organized religion and the sacraments is something temporary. It belongs to our brief era in history, the period between the first and second comings of Christ. In spite of the fact that at Benediction we sing "Adoremus in aeternum sanctissimum sacramentum", the sacraments are not eternal. The sacramental era only has a certain number of years to go, when it will be swept away. Just as the figures and metaphors of the Old Testament gave way to the reality of Christ, so our union with Christ by sacramental symbols will give way to a deeper union. All the sacraments in their symbolism look forward to this deeper reality which transcends them, and the ancient prayers of the Liturgy bring this out clearly. The post-Communion prayers of the ancient Sunday masses constantly speak of the Eucharist as foreshadowing or prefiguring union with Christ in eternity. It is the pledge of eternal life.

As St. Paul puts it, "Whenever you eat this bread or drink the chalice you shall show forth the death of the Lord, until he comes." What is true of the central sacrament, the Eucharist, is also true of all the others. They and the visible Church which they constitute belong to the era before the Lord comes, and in their symbolism they look forward to this coming as they look to the present and to the past.

The sacraments are the ways in which the Word of God is present to us in our present era. Taken as a system or order they are the Church and they are the presence of the Spirit of Christ in the world. For this reason they are the presence of the body of Christ in the world. The doctrine of the Church as the body of Christ is in some danger of being misunderstood. In our day there is a new, strong and entirely healthy emphasis on the Church as a community. The individualist piety which flourished in the last few centuries is giving way to a kind of thinking and a kind of praying which takes much more account of our fellowship in Christ. The liturgical revival is the culmination of this. We recognize much more clearly than I think previous generations have done that we are all interdependent. This important truth is sometimes expressed, and in fact was expressed by St. Paul in one of his early epistles (to the Corinthians), by saying that the Church is like a body. Just as in a body there are all kinds of different parts doing different jobs, yet all belong to the one body, all are necessary to the working of the one body, so in the Church there are all kinds of people doing all sorts of jobs, but every job has to do with the life of every other member because it has to do with the life of the whole body. This is roughly the same truth as is expressed by the name "Catholic". It is one of the great glories of the Catholic Church from a merely humanist point of view that there is no such thing as a Catholic type. There is no temperament especially suited to Catholicism, there is no nation or colour which is by nature Catholic. It is true you sometimes get people writing as though there were something especially European about the Church ("Europe is the Faith", and similar nonsense) but these are aberrations condemned by both the words and the deeds of the Church as a whole. Someone once said that an absolute rejection of racialism and nationalism, of theories of master races and inherently inferior peoples, is a fifth mark of the Church. In fact, however, it is just part of what is meant by the third of the traditional four marks. The Church is Catholic.

But this catholicity of the Church by which all kinds of people work together in a living unity is only a fractional part of what is meant by speaking of the Church as the body of Christ. In St. Paul's later epistles, especially in the last epistles—Colossians and Ephesians—the Church is called the body of Christ in a much more realist sense. The Church is sacramentally the body of Christ himself living by his Spirit in the world. In the Church we make, as it were, contact with Christ. He touches us in the sacraments. It is the body of

Christ, risen from the dead in glory, that is the source of the
Spirit for us; the sacraments make that body present to us.
It is true that although in the sacraments Christ touches us, we
do not touch him physically, because he is present only in so
far as he is symbolized, and our touching him is not directly
contained in any sacramental symbolism. Nevertheless the
sacramental order is the presence of the risen body of Christ
to the world, the source of his Spirit in the world.

The bodily presence of Christ in the world, as the Church,
differs from his bodily presence in heaven in that it is not a
physical but a sacramental presence. This was a point stressed
by Pope Pius XII in his encyclical on the Mystical Body. The
Church is not the body of Christ in such a way as to be identical with the person of Christ. In the Church Christ exists in the
sacraments, and sacramental acts are, of course, human acts.
Because of this sacramental character of Christ's presence, the
Church on earth is not yet in glory. In spite of her holiness she
contains sin, in spite of her unity she suffers schism. The Pope
reminds us in this connection of St. Paul's great image, in the
Epistle to the Ephesians, of the Church as the bride of Christ.
Here the Church is taking over the Old-Testament image of the
virgin mother Israel, the bride of Yahweh. We saw how this
image was fulfilled literally in Mary the virgin mother of Christ,
and we now see it as fulfilled sacramentally in the Church.

> Husbands [St. Paul says], love your wives as Christ loved
>   the Church . . .
> husbands ought to love their wives
> as their own bodies.
> For to love your wife, what is it but to love yourself?
> Nobody ever hates his own flesh, on the contrary he
>   nourishes it and takes care of it.
> This is just what Christ does for the Church, are we not
>   members of his body?

"Behold a man shall leave father and mother and shall join
himself to his wife, and they shall be two in one flesh."
This mystery is of great importance,
I say it applies to Christ and his Church.

[Eph. 5.]

Here the point of comparing the union of Christ and the Church
to marital union is precisely that man and wife cease to be two
quite separate bodies and become two persons in one flesh.
Each can say of the other's body, "This is my body", and this
is what Christ says of the Church.

In this chapter I have said nothing about the structure of
authority within the People of God. I have made no mention
of the authority of the bishops, and in particular of the Bishop
of Rome. I wanted to begin by establishing the sacramental
character of the Church. I did this in the hope of correcting a
false emphasis which can sometimes be given if we begin with
the notion of authority. The Church is sometimes seen as a
quasi-political entity constituted by a certain hierarchic structure of jurisdiction, and the sacraments are located within the
community. The objection to this view is that it obscures the
fact that the whole Church is sacramental, is itself the mystery,
is only truly visible to the eye of faith. The Church is first of
all the sacramental presence of Christ in the world and from
this it follows that there is authority and jurisdiction within it.
There will be much more to say of the authority within the
Church when I come to speak of the priesthood of the Church.

3

THE NEW CREATION

I N this chapter and ones which follow we shall be looking in some detail at the system of sacraments which constitutes the framework of the Church. Earlier on, I said that certain things which are said metaphorically of the People of God in the Old Testament are said literally of Christ; and these same expressions—"first-born son of God", "priest of Yahweh" etc.—are to be said sacramentally of the new People of God, the Church. The Church is Christ existing sacramentally in the world; existing, that is, in our hearts by means of the system of sacraments.

It is common to treat of each sacrament as fulfilling some particular spiritual need of a man or as corresponding to some phase of his natural life. In what follows we shall use a rather different method. We shall try to understand each sacrament by seeing what part it has to play in the realization of the Church. In the sacraments, to make the Church present and to make Christ present is one and the same thing. Denial of the real presence of the body of Christ in the Eucharist follows naturally from a denial of the real presence of the body of Christ which is his Church.

We shall begin our examination of the sacramental system by taking a look at baptism. In all the sacraments we have to distinguish between the actual sacramental sign itself and the ritual with which this sign is surrounded. The ritual is something that has slowly grown up in the course of ages and it varies from one part of the Church to another. In its attendant ritual a baptism or a mass or a marriage in the Roman rite differs from one in an Eastern rite. In its origins this ritual is simply a matter of illustrating or explaining the meaning of the sacramental sign itself, and over the centuries the explanations have become standardized to form a definite rite. The rite is not simply a matter of words spoken; the symbolism of the sacrament is also developed and explained by additional signs and symbols. For example, the sacrament of baptism makes us members of the Church; one of the ways in which this is brought home to those participating is by beginning the ceremony outside the church and moving by stages into the building during the ceremony. In innumerable ways the central sacramental symbol has been enclosed within further symbols and signs intended to elucidate its meaning. Inevitably these secondary signs and symbols are themselves sometimes in need of elucidation, and so the thing goes on. The purpose of all liturgical reform is to make these traditional explanations of the Church as lucid and clear as possible. We try to disentangle and simplify so that the proclamation of faith that the sacrament makes is not obscured by a hedge of elaborate and unintelligible ceremony. The task is, of course, one of some delicacy, for to oversimplify is to lose some of the riches which the Church has slowly gathered in centuries of penetration into the meaning and implications of the sacramental symbolism. In general the Church is reluctant to lose any of her ancient ceremonies until they can be shown to be definitely misleading to a later age. We shall have something to say later about these surrounding rites but we must begin at the centre of the sacrament with the actual sacramental sign itself.

In my first chapter I suggested that sacramental symbolism has the same structure as the sacred history of the Chosen People. In biblical history we have first of all events which are themselves significant, and then on top of that we have words, the words of the Bible which make the symbolism more precise, which highlight the point of the significance. Similarly in the sacraments there is always some significant gesture or thing, and then there are words which bring out the point of the symbolism. These are called respectively the *matter* and the *form* of the sacrament; these terms we owe to the medieval theologians, and they can be rather misleading. It is important to see that the form of words does not simply impose all the significance on the gesture; much is already there, the purpose of the words is to make it more explicit. Nor should we think of the words as defining a single simple significance and excluding all other symbolism. What the form of a sacrament does is to organize the symbolism of the matter so that we see first things first. It picks out the central point but it leaves it surrounded by other secondary interpretations.

In baptism the matter consists in the gesture of plunging under water and emerging, the form consists of the words spoken by another: "I baptize thee in the name of the Father and of the Son and of the Holy Spirit." Let us have a look at the matter first. What is the significance of this gesture? We might answer by saying that the significance is told us in the words of the form, but as I have said the function of the words is to organize a symbolism already contained in the gesture. In the matter of the sacraments there are several levels of symbolism. In the first place there is what we might call the natural symbolism of certain gestures. Man is a symbol-making creature. He rarely looks at the world in cold blood, he tends always to see a human meaning in things. It is the business of physical science, it seems to me, to correct this tendency so that we do not see simply a human meaning in, say, a tree, but also an arboreal meaning. It is the business of the scientist to see things for what they are in themselves, not for what they are to man. But it looks as though the health of the human mind requires that we should have both kinds of vision; primitive peoples in general seem to fall short on the scientific approach and I suppose most people would say that our present Western culture falls short on the poetic side. As he becomes better able to control his world man has made it more and more of a lonely and inhuman place. Nevertheless, the human meaning of things can never be entirely stamped out of man's mind; it finds its last refuge in dreams and in the whole field of behaviour that we call irrational. Whether or not we want to talk about the unconscious mind and whether or not we accept the idea of certain archetypal symbols which are common to all men, it does seem to be the case that a certain type of human meaning attaches for nearly everybody to certain things and gestures. This is what I mean by their natural symbolism. It is because they make use of these natural symbols that the sacraments can have a healing effect on the human psyche as well as their principal effect of bringing us the Spirit of Christ. They fulfil, if they are properly performed, the same psychic needs as are fulfilled by the rituals of a primitive people or by the work of the psychiatrist.

But it would be a mistake to see the symbolism of the sacraments simply in these natural terms. Besides their natural symbolism there is also the significance which the things and gestures have acquired by their use in sacred history, and so on top of what I have called natural symbolism there is something we might call biblical symbolism. When I say "on top of" here I do not mean that we have two quite separate meanings in the one gesture. What the Bible does is to take something in its natural symbolism and deepen and specialize its meaning. So in any sacramental sign you have, so to speak, a wide basis of natural symbolism, within which you have a biblical symbolism derived from its use in Scripture, and finally the whole thing is brought to sharp focus by the form of the sacrament itself.

Now what about baptism? The natural symbolism of water is tied up with creativity and new life, and this in two different ways. On the one hand water is seen as bringing new life to a thirsty land—this is the water of life, the cleansing water, the spring of living water and so on. On the other hand water has a special part to play in another kind of creation myth; here water is either the female element which is fertilized to bring forth the world, or else it is chaos, the enemy which is slain to produce the order of creation. These last two myths are in fact variants of the same theme. In the best-known Middle-Eastern creation myth the male god Marduk attacks the female dragon of the sea, Tiamat, and divides her with his sword; her blood spurts forth and from it man is made. This is the myth that lies behind part of the first creation poem in Genesis, as the Spirit of Elohim broods over the dark waters; they become fertile, they split open—"He divided the waters"—and the world is born. The other picture of water—the spring of living water—lies behind the second creation story in Chapter 2.

Generally speaking, then, in human myth and symbol, water is the female element, the mother's womb from which we are born. We find these images in the ancient tales of primitive peoples and we find them also, according to some psychologists, in our own unconscious as manifested in dreams, in poetry and so on. They represent the natural background to the symbolism of baptism, but beyond this we have the biblical symbolism. In the Old Testament creation or birth from the waters is a very important image indeed. First of all, Israel herself is born out of the waters of the Red Sea. Yahweh conquers the waters and splits them in two so that Israel can pass over into freedom. This new birth from the waters is already prefigured in the infancy story of Moses, the leader of Israel who is delivered from death by being cast into the waters and then taken from them to a new life. Again, the entry into the Promised Land marks a new era for Israel, so this story too is told with a repetition of the Exodus incidents. The River Jordan is divided and Israel marches through the waters into a new land. Finally the creation poems see the whole world as brought into being from the waters of chaos and the Flood stories tell of how all mankind was renewed by being cast on the waters like Moses (actually the word for Moses' basket is the same as that for Noah's ark), and then starting a new life.

Thus in the Bible the natural creation-symbol of plunging into water has been given a sharper edge. To the notion of creation is added that of re-creation and renewal. Noah, Moses and Israel come through the waters to a new and better life. The waters here are both the waters of destruction in which the old life dies, in which evil is cleansed away, and the waters of life from which the new life is born. The passage through the waters takes the form of a conflict, a battle in which the power of Yahweh defeats the enemies of his people. Thus already in the Old Testament plunging into water has acquired the symbolism of a victory over the enemy; the new life is a life of triumph. I suspect that this is part of the meaning of the ritual cleansing which the soldiers of Israel had to perform before they went forth to battle. The main reason for this was that battle was a sacred activity; in battle the army of Israel was the agent of the holiness of Yahweh destroying his enemies. The Hebrew soldier washed before battle as we take holy water before entering a church; it would be wrong to enter upon a holy activity in a profane state. But I suspect that besides this the washing represented a prefiguring of the result of the battle, it symbolized the triumph over the enemy, and by ritual magic made the victory more certain.

The first creation poems tells of a victory of the Spirit of God over the waters of chaos, or, if you prefer, the fertilization of the waters by the Spirit, and in the use of water symbolism throughout the Bible there is a close association between water and the Spirit. In fact living water, that is running water that sparkles and is full of life, is a common symbol of the Spirit, the life of God. In the New Testament this symbolism becomes much more explicit. For St. John the purpose of Christ's coming is to baptize in water and the Spirit. The plunging into water and rising from the water now indicates a defeat of the evil spirit by the Holy Spirit and new life in the Spirit of God.

There are three great interventions of the Spirit in the life of Christ. The first is at his conception. At the creation of the world the Spirit came down upon the waters, the female element, the mother of the world, and now at the conception of Christ, the Spirit comes down upon Mary who is to be mother of God. Secondly, at the baptism of Jesus in the Jordan, the Spirit comes down as a dove (the reference here is to the dove which intervened in the baptism of mankind in Noah). The point about this is that Jesus is beginning his public life, in which the Spirit that is in him begins to overflow from him into others. The first move in this public life is a contest with the evil spirit in which Christ is victorious. The third great intervention of the Spirit is the resurrection of Christ from the dead. He himself compares his death to the planting of a seed: "Unless the grain of wheat falls into the earth and dies it remains alone, but if it dies it brings forth much fruit." Here the mother earth has the same symbolic force as water. Jesus goes down under the earth and then rises again by the power of the Spirit to become what St. Paul calls "the first-fruits of the dead". Once again this "baptism" represents a conflict, and this time there is definitive victory. The evil spirit is defeated, death is conquered. The strange liturgy of Holy Saturday, Tenebrae, brings out this point very clearly by interweaving the themes of sleep and victory. Good Friday shows us Christ triumphant on the Cross, Holy Saturday shows him going down into the underworld, as we go down beneath the waters of sleep to encounter the unconscious forces that lie submerged in our lives. Christ goes down to carry his victory to the roots of man's being.

His victory is shown forth by his rising from the dead. He comes to life again by the Spirit and it is this new life that he pours forth into the world.

"We are buried together with Christ by baptism into death, so that just as Christ is risen from the dead by the glory of the Father, so we also may live by new life. For if we have been planted together in the likeness of his death, we shall also be in the likeness of his resurrection." (Rom. 6.45.) In this well-known passage St. Paul compares baptism to the death and resurrection of Christ, and the comparison is not an accidental one. Baptism is for each Christian a re-enactment of the Resurrection. The new birth, the new creation, which it symbolizes and makes real, is a participation in the new creation of the resurrection of Christ. Christ coming back from the dead inaugurated a new world, and by baptism we are born into this new world, the world of the Spirit. There is much more to say on this theme but for the moment I want to show how these themes— new birth, battle, resurrection, new life in the Spirit—are worked out in the ritual surrounding the central symbol of baptism. When we have looked briefly at this we shall be in a position to take stock and ask ourselves: How much does this show us of the nature of the Church?

In the first place the close connection between baptism and the Resurrection was at one time emphasized by the date at which it took place. In the early Church, baptism (except in cases of emergency) only took place once a year during the ceremony of the Easter Vigil; as a part, that is, of the celebration of Christ's resurrection, the celebration of the Christian Exodus, the creation of a new People of God. For various practical reasons this restriction no longer exists, but in the Liturgy Easter remains a feast of baptism. This is emphasized by the blessing of the baptismal font during the Vigil, and, even where there are no actual baptisms, by the new ceremony of the renewal of baptismal vows. In this ceremony I shall pick on one detail: the image of the baptismal font as the womb of Mother Church from which her children are born: "So that those who have been conceived in holiness, may come forth from the immaculate womb of the divine font, born again as new creatures, as a heavenly offspring." A parallel is here made between the baptismal font and the immaculate womb of the blessed Virgin. By the power of the Spirit the virgin mother Church brings forth Christ into the world in her children. You will remember that the celebrant takes the paschal candle, the

symbol of the risen, Christ alight with the new flame of the
Spirit, and dipping it into the water sings:

> May the power of the Holy Spirit descend into the depth of
> this font, and make the whole substance of the water fertile
> for new birth.

The fertility symbolism is here evident enough, and the sign
is completed by the priest breathing on the surface of the water
as the Spirit of God brooded over the waters at the Creation.

There is not space here to look into all the wonderful ceremonies of Holy Saturday night—the greatest celebration of
the Church's year. What I want to look at next are the ceremonies surrounding the administration of baptism. One of the
things that make these ceremonies a little difficult to follow is
that they are very much abbreviated. In fact they compress into
about twenty minutes ceremonies which used to be spread
over the whole of Lent. Lent originated as the final stage in
the preparation of catechumens for baptism, and what we have
in the present ritual of baptism are vestiges of the ceremonies
which took place week after week in preparation for the Vigil
of Easter.

At the beginning of the ceremony the candidate for baptism
is asked what he seeks from the Church of God, and he answers
"Faith". This is the key to the whole of what follows. It is
because he has faith in Christ that a man has the life of Christ
in him. Faith means a new birth, a new creation in Christ.
There follows a little ceremony which symbolizes the presence
of new life in the candidate. The priest breathes on him as God
breathed into the first man to fill him with life. It is at this
point that the symbolic contest begins, for when he breathes
upon him the priest says: "Depart from him, you evil spirit,
and give place to the Holy Spirit, the Paraclete." The battle
between Christ, the bearer of the Holy Spirit, and Satan the
evil spirit is represented again and again during the ceremony
in what are called the exorcisms. These show us that baptism

represents not merely a new birth but a victory over the powers of evil; they also indicate that the new Christian, as another Christ, will have to carry on this battle in the world. He too is to be a Christian, anointed one, a bearer of the Spirit, and in token of this he is anointed with oil. But throughout the ceremonies there is constant return to the theme of faith. Faith appears as a new wisdom, symbolized by the salt; as a reawakening of the senses, as in the anointing with spittle; but above all faith appears in the solemn proclamation of the Creed. The renunciation of Satan is complemented by an acceptance of Christ. "Dost thou renounce Satan?" asks the priest and the candidate replies "I do renounce him." It is immediately after this renunciation, this defiance of Satan, that he is anointed and comes to the font. At the font itself he passes over into acceptance of Christ. "Dost thou believe in God the Father . . . etc.?" "I do believe." "Wilt thou be baptized?" "I will." Then comes the actual sacramental sign of baptism. We do not usually plunge into water now, but it is laid down that the water must at least flow over the body, to represent a passing through the waters. The form of the sacrament, the words "I baptize thee in the name of the Father and of the Son and of the Holy Spirit", set the seal on the symbolism we have seen up to now. The new life which the candidate receives is to be life of the Trinity itself.

After the sacramental sign there follows a ceremony of great importance, the anointing with chrism; this symbolizes an important effect of baptism which we shall be saying more about in a moment—the effect that we call "baptismal character". It is followed by two ceremonies of lesser importance whose symbolism is extremely clear. The candidate puts on a white garment, to indicate the new life of grace which is his, and he carries a lighted candle in token of the victory of light over darkness. It is his personal paschal candle, symbolizing that he too has come from death to new life.

This account of the sacrament of baptism has necessarily been very superficial, but even from what has been said we can see something of what the Church must be. The Church, we may say, as a first shot, consists of those who are baptized. And what does this imply? It means, to put it as briefly as possible, that the Church is the new creation. She is not just a group of people within the world, she is a new world. The sacramental world which we enter through baptism is a distinct new creation dating from the time of Christ's resurrection. Secondly, the Church is the fellowship of faith, for faith is the first effect of baptism. Faith is the beginning of the new life in the soul; it is the reality which is symbolized and brought about by the sacrament. Faith is a divinely given response to the word of God, and in what we may call normal circumstances this faith is expressed as it is in the baptismal ceremony by the proclamation of the Creed. It is thus that St. Peter first gives expression to his union with Christ: "Thou are the Christ, the Son of the living God." Every statement of the Christian faith is an account of what this implies. I say "in normal circumstances" because the condition of the man who receives faith may be such as to prevent this kind of proclamation: If he happens to be deaf and dumb and illiterate he will not be able to show that he has the Faith in this way. Similarly a lunatic or a baby cannot proclaim the Faith immediately, though a baby can do so when he grows up. Again, an ignorant man may not be able to proclaim his faith accurately; he may miss bits out or put bits in through sheer lack of information. Thus various kinds of defect on the part of the subject may interfere with what is normally the characteristic expression of faith; and this inability to proclaim the Creed is not incompatible with the presence of faith. What would be incompatible would be a proclaimed denial of the Creed. It is one thing to be unable to affirm, is is quite another thing to deny. Thus if a man actually denies any part of the Christian faith it is impossible to baptize him. Baptism is not magic; it will not give the Faith to one who rejects it. Such a baptism would be play-acting, a pretence, and not a sacrament at all. It is important to see that it is denial of the Faith, and not just wickedness, that invalidates a baptism. A man whose heart is full of hatred but who does not deny the Creed can be genuinely baptized and receive the Faith, though in such a case the Faith he receives is what we have called "dead faith", a faith which is not enlivened by charity.

Now notice that when the candidate comes for baptism he is asked "What do you seek *from the Church of God?*" and he answers, "Faith." Faith is something he receives from the Church. It is the Church which will baptize him and so it is the Church which will tell him how to proclaim the Faith. A Church which is constituted by baptism must be the custodian of faith. It is for the Church to say whether or not some statement amounts to a denial of the Faith such as to invalidate a baptism. This in fact is thought to be the origin of the first Christian creeds. They were formulae to be recited by the candidates for baptism. The Church is not an advisory body on the sacrament of baptism, but is constituted by it. She does not therefore just give her opinion on what constitutes the Faith; she must know with certainty. With the same kind of infallible sureness with which the sacrament confers the grace of faith, the Church must be able to define what does and what does not constitute the proclamation of that faith.

To repeat the argument: Baptism is not magic; it is a human thing and the least it requires is that the recipient does not actually deny the Faith which it gives him. The Church therefore which is constituted by the sacrament must at least be able to say what would count as such a denial. It is, of course, the Church as a whole, not the individual Christian, who must be able to do this. It is the Church which is wholly constituted by the sacraments, not the individual man. As I have said, an individual may for a variety of reasons be unable to proclaim his faith adequately, or at all. The doctrine of the infallibility of the Church is just the statement that *this* kind of defect cannot overtake the Church as a whole.

I keep speaking about the Church as a whole, and you may well ask what I mean by this. How are we to know the faith of the Church as a whole? We must be able to know this, otherwise the sacrament of baptism becomes mere magic. Consideration of the sacrament of baptism simply by itself in isolation from the rest of the sacraments and from its liturgical surroundings does not, I think, give us the answer to this. The faith of the whole Church might be discovered in a variety of ways. Certain kinds of people might have special charismatic powers which enabled them to assert what the teaching of the Church is, there might be meetings in which God would endow the majority with the power of defining correctly the Christian faith, there might be an oracle which could be consulted . . . there are all sorts of possibilities in the abstract. In fact, as we shall see when we look at more of the sacraments, the Church has a definite structure which enables us to answer this question.

This is already clear from the liturgical surroundings of baptism. In the early Church it was the business of the bishop to baptize, just as it was his business to expound the Scriptures. The Church, being constituted by visible symbols, the sacraments, is a visible fellowship. In one clear sense you can count the members of the Church. They are all the people who have been baptized and who have not renounced their faith. This visibility is the visibility of the sacrament and is dependent upon the eye of faith. This is a point which has sometimes been misunderstood. When we say that the Church is visible we do not mean that everyone can see her for what she is. We are not referring to the outward things which are equally visible to everybody—some details of her organization and so on—the things that give her, according to an American estimate, a business efficiency equal to that of the Ford Company.

When the unbeliever looks at baptism he does not see the operation of the Spirit and hence he does not see the Church. But the sacraments make the Spirit of Christ visible to the Christian; that is what they are for. When the Christian and the non-Christian look at the Church they see different things.

Associated with the visibility of the Church is her visible cult, the liturgical worship that she offers to the Father. In order to understand this cult there is one further thing we must say about baptism. This sacrament, like those of confirmation and order, imparts what we call a "character". It was one of the great achievements of St. Thomas to have worked out an impressive theology of sacramental character. Briefly, what he said was this: Character means a participation in the priesthood of Christ. By baptismal character every Christian is a priest. The very early Church refused the word "priest" to Christian ministers; they called them overseers and elders and servants, but never, so far as I know, priests. This was deliberate. The word "priest" belonged first of all to the one priest Jesus Christ, who offered the one sacrifice on Calvary. As the author of the Epistle to the Hebrews insisted, there was but one sacrifice in the Christian Church, the one which Christ had offered once and for all, so there was no need for a continuing priesthood. Apart from the person of Christ, the only other subject of the word "priest" is the whole People of God. Just as the whole of Israel in the Old Testament had been a priestly people, so the new Israel, St. Peter insists in his first epistle, is a nation of priests, a royal priesthood. Because it shares in the life of Christ, because it is Christ sacramentally, the Church shares the priesthood of Christ. The Church is able to offer sacramentally the sacrifice which he offered physically on Calvary.

When the Church felt that she had made her point against the Jews and pagans, that she was different from them in not having a class of priests in their sense, when the need for distinguishing herself in this way was gone, she became less finicky in her language and allowed the use of the word to those whose priesthood was of a special kind. That is, briefly, those whose priesthood was exercised in ways that are themselves sacramental. Although all Catholics at Mass offer the Mass together, although all are priests, there is a difference in the way in which the celebrant offers and the way in which the congregation offer. Of this more will be said later—for the moment the important thing is that all are priests, and this they owe to their baptismal character.

This point about baptismal character is important when we try to draw a boundary around the Church, to say who is in it and how. There is, to my mind, no simple formula which expresses what membership of the Church is, although we can start from the on-the-face-of-it formula that the Church consists of those who are baptized and have not renounced their faith. Those at least are members of the Church in a clear and simple sense. The complications begin because of a principle that the characteristic grace which a sacrament gives us can also be received by one who *desires* to receive the sacrament but is in some way or other prevented. Thus the grace of faith is not something that waits on actual baptism. It was generally assumed in the early Church that an adult catechumen already had the Faith before he was baptized; thus he would be saved even though some accident prevented the ceremony of his baptism. He was thought to have the Faith and therefore was admitted to the readings of the Scriptures, but because he had not yet been baptized he was not admitted to the sacramental sacrifice of the Mass. The reason for this was that, although he had the Faith he did not yet have the priesthood of Christ, he could not yet offer the sacrifice with those who had been baptized. And since the early Church saw no point in the presence of mere spectators at the mysteries these catechumens were excluded.

Now there are many things which may exclude a man from baptism besides being run over by a bus. He may have what

God sees to be an inchoate desire for baptism—a desire in its most general terms for renewal in the spirit—while being impeded from baptism by the simple fact of never having heard of it. Such a man would receive the new life which baptism gives without being baptized, though he would not receive baptismal character. Now, are we to say that such people are members of the Church? It seems to me that this is a question which has no simple answer. Instead of adjusting our definition of the Church so that we can say either Yes or No, we should, I think, have a clear definition of what is manifestly the Church and then say that such and such different classes of people have a certain relation to the Church, and leave it at that. All such people are, of course, saved through the Church, and are members of it in that sense at least. It is their desire, however implicit, for membership, for baptism, which saves them. This is the meaning of the adage "Outside the Church there is no salvation." Whoever is saved is saved in virtue of his union with the Church, though that union may take a variety of different forms. The members of the Church are those who, having been baptized, do not renounce their faith—but what is it to renounce the Faith? Every child who is baptized is baptized a Catholic, no matter who baptizes him and where it happens. If he is brought up in a non-Catholic household we speak of him later as a non-Catholic. But it is usually difficult to say that such a child has actually renounced the Faith. Could there not be here mere ignorance, as in the case of many who are brought up in Catholic households and yet know next to nothing of the Faith? It seems to me that once baptized you cannot cease to be a Catholic except by the formal *sin* of heresy, and this is a very different thing from professing heretical opinions. Any Catholic may at some time hold heretical opinions through ignorance or bad instruction; the ignorance may be more or less culpable but it does not have to amount to the actual sin of heresy. Now, can we pretend that even a minority of, let us say, Anglicans who have been brought up in a wholly Anglican environment have committed the formal sin of heresy? If we think that they have not done so then we are claiming that they are Catholics just as we are—uninstructed Catholics no doubt, but frequently enough so are we. We should, to my mind, look upon the vast majority of non-Catholic Christians in this country simply as fellow Catholics who have the misfortune to be deprived of the full sacramental life of the Church. The body of Christ is the visible historical Roman Catholic Church—there can be no doubt that this is the teaching of the Church; but there may be many invisible ways of being united to it. The man who professes some peculiar heretical opinion does not look like a member of the Church, but he may be so for all we know, for his error may not be due to the sin of heresy. Even the man who has never been baptized may yet have received the grace of baptism through some hidden desire for the sacrament. But it is exceedingly important to emphasize that these links with the visible Church *are* invisible. When we speak of these things we are speaking only of what may be the case; we have no means of telling whether it is the case, for only God knows this. We know who are visibly members of the Church, and as to the rest we cannot tell, for they lie outside the sacramental sphere and only the sacraments make the Spirit visible to us. It is perhaps worth pointing out here that we are talking about the invisibility of various kinds of link with the Church, not about that other invisibility, the invisibility of a "state of grace". To guess of that many apparent non-Catholics are in reality members of the Church is by no means the same as guessing that they have charity within them. For while it is impossible to love God in charity unless we are in some way linked with the Church, it is all too possible to be linked with the Church, visibly or invisibly, and yet not to love God.

It is, of course, one thing to hold the opinion that a great many of or even all the living members of, say, the Anglican Church, are in fact, though not apparently, members of the

Catholic Church, and quite another thing to hold that the Anglican Church is a part of the Catholic Church. The Anglican Church is a venerable institution with a long history of service to Christ in this country. If England is still a Christian country we owe it primarily not to the minority who are visibly Catholics but to the faith and devotion and sheer hard work of the priests and ministers and layfolk of non-Catholic Churches. Nevertheless these organizations are not parts of the Church. The Anglican Church may provide the circumstances in which a man is saved, it may and surely does provide an immense amount of help to the Christian, but it does not save him. Nobody is saved *precisely* because of his membership of the Anglican Church; everyone who is saved is saved because of the link he has with the one Catholic Church.

There is a special class of Christians who belong visibly to the Church in the sense of having a true sacramental life and yet who are cut off from the centre; these are the schismatics. The problems raised both by schismatics and by the Protestant Churches we shall have to leave until we take a look at the sacrament of order later on. For the moment we have made a beginning of seeing how the Church is defined and constituted by the sacrament of baptism; she is a new creation, a new world brought into existence in each of us by the life of faith which we receive from "the immaculate womb of the divine font".

4

THE EUCHARISTIC COMMUNITY

I N the last chapter we spoke of the Church as the community of those who have been baptized. It is the new creation consisting of those who have left behind their old
out-of-date lives in the waters of baptism and been born again
to a new life, a share in the life that Christ brought back from
the dead. In this chapter we shall look at the Church from
another point of view. Last time we said that roughly speaking
the Church consists of those who have been baptized and have
not renounced their faith; this time we start from the rough
generalization that the Church consists of those who go to
Mass. Last time we found that the formula we started from
had a lot more in it than immediately met the eye, and we shall
find the same in this case, but once more we shall begin with
the obvious straightforward meaning and leave the qualifications until later.

It is quite easy to see what happens in a baptism; it obviously has to do with water and some kind of ritual cleansing.
Even in the hurried ceremony done in a corner of the church
on Sunday afternoon while most of the parish is sleeping off
its lunch, the onlooker can grasp what is being done. The difficulty for him may be to understand the meaning of what is
being done. The imagination crippled by our educational
methods may fail to respond to the symbolism with which
it is presented. The problem with the Mass is the opposite.
Here the difficulty is to see what is going on. Once a man has
grasped that the Mass is the sacred meal that Christians eat in
common, he has little difficulty in beginning to understand its
meaning; the ceremony of eating together is one that persists
in modern society. The difficulty even for the Catholic is that

the Mass does not really look like a common meal at all, and if you suggest to a stranger who has been to Mass for the first time that he has been attending a meeting at which the local Christians come together to eat and drink, he will be deeply puzzled. To all appearances the Mass is a secret rite conducted by a priest set apart by his special clothing and his position facing away from the audience, speaking sacred words in a beautiful and ancient hieratic language unknown to the people. At one point in the ceremony some of the people are privileged to approach the holy place to receive from the priest a private share in his mysteries; they return to their places with bowed heads and half-closed eyes, oblivious of those around them.

I do not say that this is how the Mass should appear to people, just that this is how it does appear, not only to non-Catholics but to Catholics as well and in particular to children. Children have a primitive and pagan love of the arcane and hieratic, they delight in secrets and magic and other things contrary to the life of the Christian community. It is the business of education to help the child to grow gradually out of his primitive responses to his parents and others into a mature responsible love, and it is the business of religious education to watch over the child as he transcends the magical relationship with Christ and enters into a more adult union. Of course a child of four may be a saint in his own primitive way, and of course religious education must be overwhelmingly concerned with the child's love of God here and now, but the child here and now is growing and it is our business not to hold him back but to walk beside him as he moves to more complex and more human responses to grace. It is difficult to resist the impression that the Mass in its present setting is in some ways especially appropriate to the child's vision of God rather than the adult's. Children are of course bored in church to the point of tears, but the secrecy of the thing, its unintelligibility, its remoteness, is something they do not begin to question. The fact that the Mass seems in this respect designed for children may be one reason why they stop going when they grow up.

For the moment, however, I do not want to talk about how the Mass may be made to look more like what it is, I merely want to stress that unless we see it first of all as the common meal of the Christian community we miss an essential element. The "natural" symbolism of eating and drinking is well understood in our own day. When you invite a friend into your home you offer him a drink, if it is only a cup of tea, and more formally, when you spend an evening with friends you have them in for coffee or for a meal or you go with them to the pub or you take them out to dinner. We take it for granted that food and drink cement a human relationship. Wherever two or three are gathered together in friendship there will normally be food or drink in the midst of them. The reasons that lie behind this are not difficult to see. There is a difference in kind between a gift of food and any other gift. If I give you a cigarette or a new tie I am giving you something that will please you, but when I pass you the potatoes I am giving you life. We *use* clothes and furniture and books, but we do not just use food, we are made out of food. All animals are made of food; when a man gives you dinner he is responsible for the existence of part of you. All bread at some level is the bread of life.

It is abnormal to eat alone as it is abnormal to live alone. Sometimes we have to snatch a quick lunch at a cafeteria, we sit by ourselves at the counter and get through it, but we do not reckon this a proper meal. It is an exceptional thing; there would be something inhuman about a society in which it was the norm. The normal meal, the pattern of all meals, is the family dinner or its equivalent. Here the family gather together round the same food; when friends are invited they are brought into the family circle. In such a meal the whole group is deriving its life from the same centre. The food on the table represents the common life of the family. As a general rule the head of the family from whom all have received their existence is the host from whom they receive their food. When a child is sent away from the table for misbehaving he is distressed not primarily because he is hungry but because he immediately sees this as an alienation, a being cut off from the community. Excommunication is like being sent to bed without supper. The food and drink, then, symbolize the unity and common life of the family, and this symbolism extends from the family table to nearly all other occasions of eating and drinking. Most men in a pub are, as they say, "in company", which means that you cannot buy one man a drink without being received into his group and engaging in the rather expensive ritual of giving and receiving rounds.

This natural symbolism of eating and drinking is thoroughly exploited in the Scriptures. We have already seen, in the first chapter, that the Word of God by which the Hebrews were welded into one people was represented as bread: "Not by bread alone does man live but by every word that comes forth from the mouth of God." The unity of Israel was established at the Exodus and every year they celebrate their unity, their existence as one people, by eating together the paschal meal in commemoration of the Exodus. The life they draw together from the unleavened bread and the paschal lamb symbolizes the life they first drew from Yahweh when they were reborn out of the darkness of Egypt.

There is no need to labour the symbolic significance of bread in the Scriptures, but it may be worth while looking for a moment at the use of the image of wine or the vine. Like the waters which can be both life-giving and destructive, wine has a double significance in the Old Testament. As a manifestation of the sacred, the divine power, it can "rejoice the heart of man" or it can work his destruction:

These also reel with wine
and stagger with strong drink;
the priest and the prophet reel with strong drink,

they are confused with wine,
they stagger with strong drink;
they err in vision,
they stumble in giving judgement.
For all the tables are full of vomit, no place is without
filthiness. [Isa. 28.7 ff.]

Wine is a symbol of the sacred and as such it comes to be used
as a symbol of the great manifestation of Yahweh's power in
history, his chosen people. Already Hosea rebukes the idolatry
of Israel:

Israel is a luxuriant vine
that yields its fruit.
The more his fruit increased
the more altars he built . . . [Hos. 10.1.]

But the best-known prophetic use of this image is Isaiah's
love-song of the vineyard:

My beloved had a vineyard
on a very fertile hill.
He digged it and cleared it of stones,
and planted it with choice vines;
he built a watchtower in the midst of it,
and hewed out a wine vat in it;
and he looked for it to yield grapes
but it yielded wild grapes . . .
For the vineyard of Yahweh of hosts
is the house of Israel,
and the men of Judah
are his pleasant planting;
and he looked for justice,
and behold, bloodshed;
for righteousness,
but behold, a cry. [Isa. 5.1 ff.]

The comparison of Israel with the vineyard or the vine becomes
a commonplace of later writing:

> Thou didst bring forth a vine out of Egypt
> thou didst drive out the nations and plant it.
> Thou didst clear the ground for it;
> it took deep root and rilled the land.
> The mountains were covered by its shade,
> the mighty cedars with its branches;
> it sent out its branches to the sea,
> and its shoots to the river. [Ps. 80.]

The same image is used of the Israel to come in the "Apocalypse of Isaiah":

> A pleasant vineyard, sing of it
> I, Yahweh, am its keeper;
> every moment I water it.
> Lest anyone harm it,
> I guard it night and day . . .
> In days to come Jacob shall take root
> Israel shall blossom and put forth shoots,
> and fill the whole world with fruit.

When Jesus tells his parables of the vineyard in which it is
an image of the Kingdom of God (Matt. 20 and 21, Mark 12,
Luke 20), he can rely on his hearers having these Old-
Testament passages in their minds; to them it is perfectly clear
that the kingdom of which he speaks is the vineyard of the
new messianic Israel. A more startling use of the image comes
in St. John's account of the Last Supper:

> I am the vine
> you are the branches.
> He who remains in me and I in him
> bears much fruit . . . [John 15.5.]

Here Jesus is claiming to be, himself, the new Israel. Just as he takes upon himself the titles (Christ, Son of God etc.) which originally were applied to the whole people,[1] so he now describes himself by an image that belongs traditionally to the community. He is the unity of the new People of God; it is by being united with him that we form the new community.

So by the time the bread and wine come to be used in the Eucharist they have already acquired a profound meaning. Not only do they mean ordinary human community, but they mean just that unity which has been given to the People of God; they stand for the links which are to bind together the Israel which is to come.

We are now in a position to see how the scriptural symbolism which has built upon the natural significance of bread and wine is completed by the sacramental words. Taking the symbols of what is to constitute the unity of the new Israel, Jesus says of them: "This is my body . . . this is my blood." It is his own body and blood that is to constitute the People of God; they are to form one people just in so far as their bodies are linked with his. We form one human race because ultimately our bodies are linked with those of our common ancestors, we belong to the new human race because our bodies are linked with the risen body of Christ.

There can be no doubt that in recent centuries the physical bodily aspect of our beliefs has been heavily played down. Partly because of some philosophical mistakes, we have got into the habit of thinking of the real person as an invisible immaterial being. Bodily actions are thought to be at best merely manifestations of the real human acts which take place invisibly. Thus we have tried to make morality merely a matter of motives and intentions and other "acts of the mind"; physical acts have been thought of as morally good or bad only in virtue of their relationship to these interior acts. In a parallel

---

[1] See Chapter 2.

way some people have tried to make of heaven a "state of mind"; the emphasis has been all on the immortality of the soul, while the primary Christian teaching on the resurrection of the body has been pushed well into the background. It is only in comparatively recent years that Christian thinkers have returned to a more traditional way of thinking about man.

In the first place it seems clear that since Christ is a man it is only possible to be present to him in a human way by physical bodily presence. God does not need a body in order to be present to us, for he is present in a divine way, but a man without a physical body can only be absent from us—this is what bereavement means. To be present to another man we have either to be in the same place, where we can see and hear and touch each other, or else to be linked indirectly by some means involving our bodies, by a phone call or a letter. However much two lovers who are parted may think of each other, they remain in fact parted until there is some physical link between them, a link which in the natural order is most perfect when they are two in one flesh. If Christ were not a living body he would be humanly absent from us, if he were dead we could remember him but we could not be in his human presence. It is precisely because he is risen from the dead that he is with us:

"Resurrexi, et adhuc tecum sum."

It is our presence to the risen Christ that makes us one community; the Eucharist and the sacraments that surround it constitute the Church. Of course we are not in the Eucharist present to the body of Christ by being in the same place or by making the sort of direct physical contact that we can make with other people in the same room; the body of Christ, as the Council of Trent reminds us, is not present in the Eucharist naturally but sacramentally; nevertheless, there is a genuine human presence involving our bodies and his. All this would, of course, fall to the ground if we lost our hold on the real bodily presence of Christ, if we thought of the Eucharist in psychological terms as merely making an appeal to our minds—reminding us of a person no longer with us.

The unity of the new Israel is the body of Christ, but it is his consecrated body, his sacrificed body, his glorified body. The unity of the Church, he says, "is my body given for you . . . is the new alliance in my blood, shed for you". It is through the shedding of his blood that his body becomes the foundation of the new creation. This is because the shedding of his blood is a sacrifice, literally a making-sacred. It is his passing over from the old world to a new. It is St. John above all who insists on this point; the mission of Jesus is only fulfilled by his being "lifted up" by his return to the Father, by his being glorified.

> He spoke of the Spirit which was to be received by those who believed in him; for there was as yet no Spirit since Jesus had not yet been glorified. [John 7.39.]

> Behold the hour has come
> when the Son of Man is to be glorified.
> Amen, Amen, I say to you,
> if the grain of wheat does not fall into the ground and die
> it remains alone;
> if it dies
> it bears much fruit. [John 12.23–5.]

Western tradition has concentrated so much on the passion of Christ that we are in danger of forgetting that the essential point of it was not the heroic endurance of sufferings but the passing over from the world of corruptible flesh to the new world of his immortal risen body. It is in this consecration of his body that his sacrifice essentially consists.

Sacrifice means taking something out of its profane use and bringing it into the sphere of the sacred. The people take some animal or other object which represents themselves and by making it sacred they come themselves within the range of the divine. Frequently the identification with the sacred object is completed by a ritual meal. It should be remembered, of course, that in primitive and Christian societies all meals are more or less sacrificial; the food and drink are first dedicated to God and become to some degree sacred.

Such is the state of the fallen world that the profane and the sacred are at odds with each other. There is no simple transition from one to other, the movement is a dialectic in which we can only transcend the profane by denying it. It is for this reason that sacrifice at its most characteristic involves death, the total renunciation of the profane world; the grain of wheat must die before it can bring forth new life. It is for this reason that the sacrifice of Christ involves his death and that is why in the Eucharist in which we are present to the risen body of Christ, we "show forth his death". (1 Cor. 11.26.)

In its form the Mass is first of all the sacrifice of the Church, though it only becomes perfectly the sacrifice of the Church as it becomes the sacrifice of Christ. We take bread and wine, symbols of the common life of the people, and we offer them to God—that is to say, we make them sacred, consecrate them to the divine sphere. The dedication of the bread and wine represents the dedication of our lives to God. But the bread and wine come to represent our common life most perfectly just when they come to represent sacramentally the body of Christ, because fundamentally our common life is life in the body of Christ. The Mass is not two things: the sacrifice of the Church and the sacrifice of Christ. From one point of view it is the sacrifice of Christ because it is the sacrifice of the Church—for the Church's sacrificial meal, the "breaking of bread", is the sacramental rite which shows forth and realizes the sacrifice of Christ. From another point of view it is the sacrifice of the Church only because it is the sacrifice of Christ, for it is only in Christ that the Church realizes herself; until the bread and wine represent Christ they do not at the deepest level represent us.

We have become accustomed over the past few centuries to thinking of the Mass primarily as the re-presentation of Calvary. We think of it first of all as making Christ and his sacrifice present. We should think of it also, and perhaps first of all, as making the Church present and her sacrifice. For the Church is not present merely because her members are together in one room. It is not their bodily presence to each other that fundamentally links them, but their common bodily presence to the risen body of Christ. The Eucharist and the sacraments in general make Christ present, but they do this in the act of making the Church really present. This fact, that the Church is only fully present in the sacramental life, can be obscured by our tendency to think of the Church as an organization visible and patent to all. It is true that she is visible even to the unbeliever, but she is a mystery and all that the unbeliever sees is the outer fringe of things. It is only the believer, who sees the sacraments for what they are, who sees the Church as she really is.

But, as we saw in the previous chapter, although the believer can see into the sacraments to the reality of the Church, it is not given to him to see all the members of the Church. There are those who are united to the Church by links which are not made sacramentally visible even to the eye of faith. Besides the comparatively small group of men who are actually gathered at the eucharistic meal there may be many more who are united with them invisibly, men and women whose lives are a sharing in the sacrifice of Christ but who through no fault of theirs are absent from its sacramental enactment. Here the all-important principle to remember is that those who with a will moved by divine grace sincerely desire to receive a sacrament, but are prevented from doing so, share fully in the ultimate effect of that sacrament, the growth of charity. We should particularly remember this when we think of the worship of other Christians. It is in their prayer and especially in their common prayer that they most fully express their invisible union with the sacramental Church, and for this reason the services of other Christian communities may be for them the occasions of that same eucharistic grace which we receive at Mass. However clear we may be that their worship is not the Mass, that Christ's body is not sacramentally present on their altars, it is if anything more important to be clear that his Spirit is present in those who sincerely believe that they are taking part in the act of Christian worship. The reason why we are compelled to say that some Christian worship is not in fact the Mass is something we shall be talking about in the last chapter, when we come to discuss the differing roles of laity and sacramental priesthood in the offering of the sacrifice.

5

PENANCE, FIRST OF THE SACRAMENTS
OF RETURN

IN this chapter and the next I want to say something about the sacraments of penance and the anointing of the sick. What I have to say is more than usually tentative; where it differs from what is more commonly taught it should be regarded as an attempt to throw additional light on the topic, not to supplant accepted ways of thought.

First I must explain why I treat these two sacraments together: it is because I regard each of them as a sacrament of return to the Eucharist. Each of them belongs to a situation in which the Christian is for one reason or another prevented from sharing fully in the Mass. Penance deals with the obstacles created by sin, anointing with those due to sickness. As I have suggested earlier, we get the clearest view of any sacrament when we see how it is eucharistic, how it is related to the common meal that symbolizes Christian love. To see how a sacrament—or anything else for that matter—belongs to the Eucharist is to see its function in the Church; for the Church is centred upon the Lord's Supper.

The anointing of the sick has for a long time been treated as a sacrament of the dying. Its commonest name, "extreme unction" (surely the most atrocious latinism in the English language), suggests that it belongs to the end of life. Historians of dogma have come to recognize in modern times that this was not its original function and theologians nowadays most commonly treat it as a sacrament to help the sick, rather than as an immediate preparation for death.[1] The true sacrament of

---

[1] For an excellent treatment of this question in English see Charles Davis, *The Study of Theology*, London, Sheed and Ward (1962), pp. 276–98.

the dying is the Viaticum, the last communion in sacrament before sharing in the banquet of heaven. In these chapters I shall be taking it for granted that the anointing of the sick is not immediately a preparation for death but a preparation for Mass. It is directed, I believe, neither towards a purely invisible condition of the soul nor towards physical health as such, but as is clearly stated in the liturgy of the sacrament, towards a return to Christian worship.

When we see penance and anointing as similar in this way, as parallel paths of return to the Eucharist, they throw light on each other. What is obvious in one is suddenly seen to be present in the other too. It becomes apparent that each is a kind of resurrection, each a struggle with Satan, each a rejoining of the community, and we recall that all these are themes of baptism. In this way the general pattern of life in the Church becomes more intelligible.

The Church exists, as I have explained earlier on, at the sacramental level, a sort of intermediate level between the obviously visible and the purely interior and personal. The ancient analysis of a sacrament is, I have suggested, an analysis of the Church in our present era between the first and second comings of Christ. There is first the sacramental rite (*sacramentum tantum*), something that is visible to believer and unbeliever alike. Then there is, within this, a reality known only by faith and inaccessible to the unbeliever, the sacramental reality (*sacramentum et res*) which we might also call the "ecclesial reality", for this is the level at which the Church has her being. Beyond this is the final reality for the sake of which the Church exists, the personal sharing in divine life that we call grace (*res tantum*).

In this chapter and the following one I shall try to analyse penance and the anointing of the sick in terms of these three levels and I hope it will be clear that this is no mere exercise in theological tidying-up. We shall be trying to see how the sacramental rite shows forth the life of the Church, how in each case the sacramental reality constitutes that life (how it is eucharistic), and how all this fosters the personal divine life of the Christian.

The sacrament of penance is concerned with sin as a barrier between a man and the Eucharistic meal. We are naturally inclined to think of sin first of all as affecting our individual relationship with God. It seems first of all to be a private affair. Once we examine the matter, however, it is evident that the relationship with God with which we are concerned is our union with him in Christ—there is no other way of being united with God. Sin cuts us off from our union in Christ and this is a union with our fellow Christians. Sin is therefore a social thing (or rather an anti-social thing) not merely in its effects but in its essence, just as charity, the opposite of sin, is a social thing in its essence. We do not love each other simply in *consequence* of loving God—as though it just happened that he had commanded it. It is, as St. Thomas says, "specifically the same act whereby we love God and whereby we love our neighbour". It is impossible to have divine love for either without the other. Sin (I speak of mortal sin) is the cessation of charity, it means that the Spirit, the life-blood of the body, no longer flows through a particular member.

Sin cuts us off from our fellow Christians first of all at the deepest level, at the level of sanctifying grace; we are no longer united with them in the invisible union of the Spirit. There are corresponding ruptures at the other two levels. Take first the level of sacramental reality. We saw in the previous chapter that the first symbolism of the eucharistic meal is friendship; we eat and drink together to show that we are united in love. We share a divine food because we share a divine friendship. From this it follows that to share in that meal when we are not united in divine love with our fellows is to tell a lie. It is not mere deception but actual lying; for to receive Communion is to make a gesture which actually proclaims something about the recipient, the most important fact about him—that he shares the life of the Trinity. The unworthy communicant is using this most solemn and sacred language to lie. Thus the isolation from his fellow men which the sinner has brought about at the deepest level is reflected at the sacramental level in the loss of the right to share in the eucharistic meal. He can no longer exercise to the full his baptismal priesthood. Finally, at the external level of sacramental rite this loss of rights may be officially proclaimed, the sort of thing that is commonly meant by excommunication.[1]

One additional point must be made clear before we try to sort out these three senses in which a sinner is cut off from the Church. I have spoken of the sinner losing his "right" to receive Communion; it should also be evident that he has lost the power to desire to receive Communion. I speak of "desire" here in the sense in which we speak of "baptism of desire"—that desire for a sacrament which of itself brings us the final fruits of grace even if the sacrament itself is for some reason not available to us.[2] The sinner cannot in this sense desire to receive Communion. To do so would be already to have repented his sin, to have ceased to be a sinner. He may of course want to go to Communion in some other sense—to avoid looking conspicuous or because he refuses to recognize his sin, but this is not the grace-motivated desire which brings with it eucharistic grace. It is important to be clear that the sinner has lost the power to desire Communion for, as we shall see, he may, by secretly repenting, recover this desire before the right to share in the meal has been restored to him.

---

[1] I use this term in a rather loose sense as I do not wish to enter into details of canon law.

[2] This "Eucharist of desire" is nowadays often called "spiritual Communion", a deplorable use of language which suggests that the actual eating of the Host is not *in itself* spiritual. St. Thomas uses "spiritual Communion" to mean reception of Communion in good dispositions as opposed to an unworthy Communion.

Suppose a Christian deliberately and publicly does something that is clearly contrary to Christ's teaching—he joins in the worship of an idol, let us say, or commands that all the people in a city should be burnt as an act of war, or orders the destruction of a whole race. Such a man, we might expect, would be excommunicated. It would be a mockery for him to take a normal part in the Christian assembly and the primary purpose of his excommunication would be to make this clear to him in the hope that it would induce him to repent.[1] Supposing the man does repent, then he will be reconciled with the community. He will show that he has repented by his willingness to submit to the authority of the community. This is one element in the concept of *"doing* penance"—it shows something; I know that I am truly repentant if I find myself prepared to put myself at the disposal of the community whose will I have previously flouted. The other element is a personal one; doing penance has an important effect on the individual who does it. Of this more later.

Now, a ceremony of reconciliation is something that you might expect to exist in any society which proclaims a way of life. If living in a certain community entails being prepared to live in accordance with norms laid down by that community, then re-entry by one who has deliberately defied these norms may be expected to involve some manifestation of submission to the authority of the community. All this, we may say, is natural enough in any such society; the special thing about the Christian community is that this ceremony of reconciliation is sacramental. Just as we saw that most communities have an initiation ceremony but in the case of Christianity baptism is a sacrament, and most groups have a common meal but the eucharistic meal is a sacrament, so most communities may be

---

[1] According to the Code of Canon Law in the Church punishment exists simply for the reformation of the man who is punished.

expected to have a rite of reconciliation, but for us it is a sacrament. Thus the external rite of reconciliation, when genuinely performed, symbolizes and brings about a reality at the sacramental level—the restoration of the right to share in the Eucharist. This, I would suggest, is the sacramental reality in penance. This in its turn symbolizes and brings about a reality of personal grace which we may describe in various ways; it is return to the invisible community of charity, it is restoration of the power to desire the Eucharist, it is *contrition.*

Before saying more about this, it is important to notice a special peculiarity of the sacrament of penance. In a sacrament such as the Eucharist or baptism the three levels of reality are so to speak separable. The external rite will only bring about the sacramental reality if it is genuinely performed (thus one can go through the motions of baptism—for example in order to make a film about the sacrament—without genuinely performing the rite. The context indicates that here there is no genuine intention to baptize). It is the absence of *pretence* that is required in order that the external rite should infallibly produce the sacramental reality. For the next stage what is required is the absence of *bad dispositions* in the recipient. Thus I may share in the sacrament of the Eucharist but it is of no profit to me if I encourage my attention to wander or positively reject the divine love it brings. It is clear that normally these two conditions, absence of pretence and absence of bad dispositions, are different things. A wicked priest can still celebrate the Eucharist without pretence and the body of Christ will be sacramentally present; on the other hand, even a saint may go through the motions of the Mass fictionally to show someone how it is done. In the case of penance, however, no such distinction is possible; in this case the actual genuineness of the rite depends on a certain good disposition.

This is because, as St. Thomas points out, the rite itself involves a personal act. The symbolic act is the actual humble request for, and granting of, forgiveness. Such a request is not genuine unless it is an expression of penitence. We should not be misled by a false dualistic psychology into thinking of the penitential disposition as something wholly private and interior and separate from the penitential behaviour of confession. If this were true there would indeed be a puzzle as to how something hidden in this way could be an element in a sacramental symbol. The truth is however that the mental act of penitence is visible, the penitential behaviour is its visibility.

In this sacrament the rite is only genuine if good dispositions are present. Hence in this sacrament there can never be the sacramental reality without the ultimate reality of grace, for either the good dispositions are present and hence the sacramental reality bears fruit in grace, or they are not present and there is no sacramental reality either.

That penitence belongs to the nature of the rite of confession should make a great deal of difference to our religious teaching. You can teach someone how to baptize or how Mass is said; it is a sort of technique. But if you teach a technique of "making a confession" you are in danger of setting up the idea that the sacrament is in some way separate from the dispositions of the penitent. To have the wrong dispositions in the Eucharist is a bad thing, to have the wrong dispositions in the sacrament of penance is an impossible thing—the sacrament would not exist. This sacrament, above all others, is a personal act. For many of our children, however, it is firstly a feat of memory and secondly a triumph of will over embarrassment. I do not know how to remedy this but it is easy to see how it is encouraged.

I have spoken of the external rite of penance as a matter of reconciling a sinner who has been officially banished from the Eucharist. The origins of our present rite are complicated and obscure but it does seem to derive from the reconciliation of public penitents on Holy Thursday. At the beginning of Lent they had appeared before the bishop and received the tokens of penitence. Our own ceremonies of Ash Wednesday and indeed the whole penitential aspect of Lent derive from this.

Throughout Lent they were obliged to leave Mass before the Offertory, besides performing certain penances to manifest the sincerity of their sorrow. On Holy Thursday they were received back into the community. In our present rite we have, so to speak, telescoped the beginning and end of Lent. The confession corresponds to the ceremony of Ash Wednesday, the absolution to the ceremony of reconciliation. Although the confessor must be sure that the penitent is genuinely sorry for his sin he does not nowadays take forty days to convince himself.

In our day, as in ancient times, the job of reconciling the penitent belongs essentially to the bishop. The penitent wishes to come back to the community and the only man who can speak for the whole community is its bishop. He, as sacramentally representing Christ in whom the Christian community is one, speaks for them as a Church, even more than would, say, their unanimous vote. It is because this function belongs to the bishop alone that a priest normally cannot give absolution without "faculties" from the bishop in whose diocese he is. Sometimes this point is put in a different way; it is said that the priest needs faculties because he must have "jurisdiction". This is indeed the normal way of speaking and, of course, it is perfectly accurate. It seems to me, however, that in an age such as ours, when the main pastoral problem about this sacrament is that so many Christians approach it legalistically, it is a pity to use language that seems to favour this outlook. What we mean by saying that the priest has jurisdiction is that he has the authority lent him by the bishop to speak and act for the whole Church in this matter. His authority is not, of course, unlimited; it extends just so far as the bishop has made it extend. It is his business to judge whether or not the sins which the penitent has committed are such that he has the authority to absolve them, and of course he may have to help the penitent to judge himself. But essentially the confessor is there to bring the mercy of Christ to his fellow men. Whatever judicial elements may be detected in his function, in actual practice the confessional is not remotely like a law-court.

I have suggested that in this sacrament the rite is the encounter between the repentant sinner and the community from which he has strayed; his submission and their welcome. The sacramental reality symbolized and effected by this rite is the restoration of the sinner to the full exercise of his baptismal priesthood; he is once more entitled to share fully in the Eucharist. This sacramental reality in its turn represents and realizes the return to the community of charity. I am suggesting that the final effect of the sacrament is perfect contrition. I shall further suggest that what is sometimes called "attrition" is just the good dispositions which we saw were necessary in order that the external rite of the sacrament should be genuine and in order that the sacramental reality should be able to bear fruit in grace. What is known as "an act of perfect contrition" should be thought of, it seems to me, as "penance by desire" on the analogy of "baptism of desire".

From these premises it would follow both that an act of perfect contrition is sufficient for the forgiveness of sin even without the sacrament of penance itself, and that attrition is sufficient for the forgiveness of sins provided that we actually receive the sacrament. On the view that I am suggesting it is quite obvious why this should be so: perfect contrition just *is* the forgiveness of sins; it is the grace of this sacrament, and the effect of this sacrament is precisely to make attrition into perfect contrition.

In the customary catechesis of this sacrament it is a great deal less clear why this should be so. We are usually given a psychological account of the difference between attrition and contrition instead of a theological one. The impression is given that the difference lies in what you are thinking about when you are sorry for your sins. If you are bothered about hell then all you have is attrition, if you can abstract yourself from such "selfish" motives and think only of the goodness of God then you may well have perfect contrition. I was once told: "Ask yourself if you would still be sorry if you knew that God would condemn you to hell all the same." Admittedly this somewhat peculiar way of meditating on the goodness of God is not representative of our teaching, but perfect contrition does tend to be presented as an especially difficult psychological feat—it is advisable to learn how to do it, in case the car skids when a priest cannot be had. I have no wish to suggest that the workings of grace are so "supernatural" as to be psychologically undetectable; I do not say that the difference between attrition and contrition is irrelevant to experience (provided we recognize the elusive character of "experience"). What I say is that their difference cannot be defined in psychological terms. Contrition is charity in particular circumstances and charity cannot be defined by introspection; it is our sharing in the life of God. If we do want to describe it in terms of experience we are on far safer ground if, like St. Paul to the Corinthians, we talk about the sort of behaviour it normally leads to, than if we try to talk about what it feels like.

We call sin "mortal" on the analogy of suicide. A living man has it in his power to kill himself; he does not need any superhuman power to reject the life he has been given. Death is, however, a one-way road; a man who has killed himself has no power to return to life. Only a miracle could raise him from the dead. It is the same way with sin; a man who lives by divine life has it in his own power to cast that life away, but once he has cast it away he has no power whatever to return to life. Just as there is nothing about a corpse which leads us to expect it to revive, so there is nothing about a sinner which would lead us to expect him to repent. When a sinner does repent it is by an intervention of God as gratuitous and uncovenanted as the raising of Lazarus. The raising of Christ from death to life is the great sacrament of the forgiveness of sin. Every repentance is a resurrection deriving from that Resurrection.

Let us be clear about the relation between repentance and forgiveness. If Fred offends Charlie and Charlie forgives him, then Charlie changes his mind about Fred. At first he was angry, now he isn't any more. But when Fred offends God and God forgives him, God does not change his mind about Fred, on the contrary he changes Fred's mind about him. The forgiveness of sin is not a change that comes over God but a change that comes over us, brought about by God. We should not think of our repentance as causing God to forgive us; our repentance and our being forgiven are two sides of the same divine gift, the gift that comes to us through the sacrament of penance. For this reason it is correct to say either that the grace of the sacrament is the forgiveness of sins or that it is contrition.

Now we have seen in connection both with baptism and the Eucharist the general principle that if a man desires to receive a sacrament but is in some way prevented from doing so he has already received the grace of the sacrament. The desire in question is of course not just *any* desire for the sacrament. A man may want to be baptized for some political reason but this would not be baptism of desire; it must be desire for the sacrament in its inner depths for its own sake. Such a desire can only itself be the effect of divine grace. It is my view that the "act of perfect contrition" is just such a desire for the sacrament of penance. Now we saw that although such desire brings the life of grace which the sacrament would bring, it does not bring the sacramental reality. Baptism of desire brings sanctifying grace, but it does not bring baptismal priesthood (or "character"); desire for the Eucharist brings an increase of charity, but does not make present the body and blood of Christ. Similarly desire for penance, although it brings forgiveness, does not restore the full exercise of the baptismal priesthood, the right to share in the Eucharist. It is for this reason that a man who is genuinely repentant may not receive Communion until he has received the sacrament of penance.

It is however of very great importance to stress the difference between "eating and drinking the body and blood of Christ unworthily"—which means receiving Communion in unrepented mortal sin—and receiving Communion after repentance when it has not been possible to go to confession. (Of course one clear indication that one has not got genuine desire for the sacrament would be not to go when it was possible.) The first of these is the sacrilegious lie of which I have already spoken, the second is clearly a much lesser evil. It is sometimes argued that if one is truly repentant one should not refrain from going to Communion even though it has not been possible to go to confession, for a man should not let something which is merely accidental cut him off from the grace of the Eucharist. It is not good enough to answer this by saying "Ah, but it is very difficult to make an act of perfect contrition; how can you be sure that you have truly repented?" A more satisfactory answer is that to produce this argument is to forget that there is such a thing as Eucharist by desire. A man who genuinely desires to receive Communion but is prevented by something outside his control (such as the unavailability of confession) has already received the grace of the Eucharist.

But whatever answer we make to such an argument we must recognize that there were long periods in the Church when the necessity for sacramental confession was not seen as clearly as we see it. The early Christians were no doubt as prone to sin as ourselves, yet so far as we can tell they did not go to confession as frequently as we do. In later centuries increasing clarity on this point seems to have expressed itself partly in increasing frequency of confession but partly also in increasing rarity of Communion. Our present understanding of the necessity of both sacraments must be reckoned a genuine development of dogma.

Greater clarity about the importance of confession has, however, been bought at a fairly stiff price. Besides a growing nervousness about sacramental Communion, there also appeared the manuals for confessors which, with their very natural concern with the classification and subdivision of sins, had a distorting effect on the theology of the Christian life. Accompanying this there has been a certain legalism and a decline in teaching about grace and the primacy of God's mercy. The general effect has been somewhat to depersonalize the moral life, and a very significant indication of this has been the tendency to regard sacramental confession as an *alternative* to perfect contrition. What I have been trying to say is that the sacrament is the source of contrition and its nourishment. Contrition is an aspect of the life of charity, it is a constant element in the Christian life; to forget this is to ignore the truth behind the Protestant thesis that the Christian is *simul Justus et peccator*—at once justified and a sinner. For the Catholic this can never mean, of course, that justification is not a real effect in us. To be forgiven is to become a different kind of being, really to share in divinity, but an essential part of the life of grace in us is the life of contrition. We are contrite not because we fear we are not yet justified, but as an expression of the fact that we are justified.

This may help us to understand the place of mortification in the Christian life. In the first place this ought not to be identified with the austerity demanded by the ordinary human virtue of self-control. A civilized man will avoid self-indulgence because it is an enemy to maturity; part of the business of growing up is finding a mean between indulgence and repression. This fact of ethics may throw some light on the Christian life but the two must not be confused. The essential difference is that self-control is concerned with living, whereas self-denial is concerned with dying.

From the point of view of the moral philosopher there will be exceptional occasions when a man, if he is to retain his dignity and decency, must choose death; we distinguish fairly sharply between heroism of this kind and suicide. The Christian knows, however, that these apparently exceptional cases form the pattern of man's vocation. What is demanded of us is that we should die in Christ; it is a matter of comparative unimportance whether we die for Christ publicly, as the martyrs do, or privately; the same giving up of life is required of us all. It is only if we relinquish our lives as Christ did on Calvary that we shall rise with him to new life.

I do not see this as in the first instance metaphorical. The first thing that is required of a Christian is that his actual physical death should be a sacrificial offering. It is in preparation for this that he metaphorically "dies to the world" during his life. This is what I called earlier the second and personal element in doing penance. In the first place doing penance as a part of the sacrament is a matter of putting yourself under the power of the community which you have hitherto defied; in the second place it is rehearsing for death. In this second aspect mortification, which goes beyond the formal demands of the sacrament of penance, is an expression of the contrition which is a permanent element in Christian life.

This sketch for a theory of penance is likely to give rise to the objection that it presents a Christianity which rejects life. The humanist has always complained that the pale Galilean teaches a fear of life; the notion that Christianity is essentially a preparation for death surely justifies this criticism. The Christian can only reject the world and human values and long to be released by death from the demands of responsible adult living. To this criticism we reply that our emphasis on death implies no devaluation of life; the death of a Christian is not an escape from but a sacrificial offering of life; we offer what we value most. The Christian holds in tension the two ideas: the importance of human achievement and the need to transcend it. The man who would identify martyrdom with suicide has himself not recognized the value of life; life draws its significance from death and without this it is trivial. In saying this the Christian is of course committed to denying that death is merely the last moment of life. For him it is the climax and the crisis. For the non-Christian death need have no more intrinsic significance than any other point in life, but we believe that since the Crucifixion death has become the way either to resurrection and new life or to rejection of this life.

What is required at death is that we abandon ourselves totally, that we accept the dissolution of all that self has meant to us. This absolute abandonment of self is something only possible to us if we live by divine life; it is the work of grace. Any other kind of self-abandonment is bogus, it ties us yet more firmly to ourselves, it is a form of suicide. This may help us to answer an obvious objection to the view I have been suggesting. If I take so literally the idea that we have to die as the martyrs do, what about those who are not conscious as they die? What about those who die suddenly with no time to think of offering their lives in sacrifice? I think we can under-stand this on the analogy of infant baptism: here we have another example of a work of grace where there is no personal act of co-operation. An infant is genuinely baptized before he himself does anything about it, but it is required of him that as he becomes capable of it, he makes the divine life in him something personally his own. In just the same way even though the act of death by which we are united with the cross of Christ should be a work of grace and no conscious act of ours, yet is it required of us that we make it personally our own. It is this personal appropriation of our death that is achieved by mortification in this life and, I would like to suggest, by purga-tory in the next.

One effect of sin is that it becomes harder for us to die. Sin, besides turning us from God, binds us closer to ourselves, so that the abandonment of self becomes more difficult. This ten-dency to self-centredness is something that may remain even when our sin is forgiven; it is eradicated only by deliberate self-denial. Self-denial, then, is not the same as self-control, nor is it the vice of excessive self-repression; self-control is the attitude of the good man towards his desires with a view to living well, while self-denial is the attitude of a man towards his desires with a view to transcending the good life. As we know, the human virtue of self-control cannot exist for long without divinely inspired self-denial, but soon degenerates into subtler forms of selfishness and pride.

It is very tentatively that I finally put forward a view of purgatory. It seems to me that we should see purgatory somewhat on the analogy of mortification rather than on the analogy of punishment (though the theory of punishment is itself so debatable that it is in any case unclear what would count as a punitive theory of purgatory). I suggest that purgatory consists in the personal appropriation of death. This immediately explains three of the main things we know about purgatory. First, that the soul in purgatory is assured of heaven; for grace has done its work, rather as in the case of the baptized infant. Second, that the more a man has sinned the more difficult purgatory is. Third, that the more a man has done penance the easier it is. There is of course the important difference between mortification or appropriation of death in this life and after death; that mortification is a voluntary anticipation of death performed for the love of God and thereby nourishing the love of God in our hearts, whereas purgatory is a matter of having to accept what is happening, and is therefore not itself meritorious.

I put forward this view of purgatory merely for discussion. It has, no doubt, serious weaknesses and at least one obvious gap. I have said nothing about what is after all the actual basis for the doctrine of purgatory: that the Church does in fact pray for the dead. The fact that we can bear one another's burdens in this way is surely an important clue to the nature of the Church. But these matters cannot be gone into here and now.

6

THE SECOND SACRAMENT OF RETURN:
ANOINTING THE SICK

I N the last chapter I suggested that the sacraments of penance and the anointing of the sick could be seen as parallel
paths of return to the Eucharist. Each of them belongs to
the situation in which a man is prevented from taking part in
the Eucharist; penance has to do with the obstacle created by
sin, anointing with the obstacle of sickness. This is not the
most widespread view of the anointing of the sick, but there
can be very little doubt that it was the ancient view of the
Church. For most Catholics "extreme unction" is associated
with the deathbed, not with healing; the very name suggests
the last moments of life. It is commonly regarded as a preparation for death, and its effect is believed to be primarily an
invisible one, though it is conceded that an improvement of
health may also follow by way of a bonus. It would probably
be said that the effect of the sacrament is "spiritual" rather
than "physical". I shall be suggesting in contrast to this that
the tradition of the Church knows no such opposition between
spiritual and bodily, and that the liturgy of the sacrament definitely suggests that it exists for spiritual bodily healing.

At the Mass of the Chrism on Holy Thursday morning the
oil of the sick is blessed so that it may "become a spiritual
ointment for strengthening the temple of the living God; so
that the Holy Spirit may dwell therein". It is clear that the
anointing is not seen as a sort of medicament; its purpose is
not simply physical health but a vitality associated with the
presence of the Holy Spirit; nevertheless, what is in question
is a bodily vitality. The liturgy of blessing goes on to pray that

all who are anointed with the oil may be "safe in mind and body, every pain, weakness and sickness of mind and body being expelled".

The words which are nowadays used during the actual anointing refer to "forgiveness" and not directly to any improvement in health, but the surrounding prayers make it clear that the aim is the recovery of the sick man:

> We beg you, our Redeemer, by the grace of the Holy Spirit to heal this sick man of the illness that afflicts him. Cure his ailments, forgive his sins, rid him of all pain of mind and body. Mercifully restore him to full health both interior and exterior, so that, made whole by your goodness, he may return once more to his work . . . Free your servant from his sickness and restore him to health. Stretch out your hand and raise him up, give him new strength and maintain him in it, give him back to your holy Church with all he needs for his well-being.

It is clear, then, that the popular view of this sacrament as a preparation for death finds no support in the actual rite. It is founded instead upon certain theological presuppositions and upon the practice of administering the sacrament only when the patient is not expected to recover. It is alleged that Christ came to save our "souls" and not our bodies and that his sacraments exist to bring us grace, which is "in" the soul; bodily health is quite accidental and of itself irrelevant to the sanctity of the soul. Moreover, it is argued, if bodily health were the effect of the sacrament, a good Christian with access to the sacrament should never die; at the very least, we should expect many more cures than we in fact find.

In, spite of these objections I shall argue that the "sacramental reality" (*sacramentum et res*) of this sacrament is a bodily condition ordered towards participation in the Eucharist, and the final personal reality of grace (*res tantum*) is a recovery or strengthening of loving desire for this participation.

In order to understand the sacrament we must first set it in its proper context of a theology of sickness founded in the Scriptures. Very little attention is paid these days to this topic. Sickness is thought to be relevant to the Christian simply as presenting certain moral problems. In this respect it has suffered somewhat the same fate as the related topics of sex and work, which have in general been treated as of purely moral interest. Roughly speaking, sickness has been presented as primarily an occasion for the exercise of Christian resignation; it is one important way in which the Christian can conform his life to the sufferings of Christ. There has even been a tendency amongst certain "spiritual writers" to regard rude health as slightly suspect; the unworldly soul, like the Victorian heroine, will be pale and liable to some complaint. That sickness can and should be an occasion for suffering in Christ is quite obviously true, but we may question whether this is the most obvious truth about it. We may begin by noticing that on no single occasion does Christ counsel a sufferer to resign himself to his sickness. In the Gospels sickness is invariably represented as an enemy, something to be defeated. I shall suggest that if we follow the thought of the New Testament we shall see sickness primarily as a temptation. Like any other temptation, it can be an occasion of the growth of charity, but this is not the first thing to be said of it. The first thing to say about temptations is that they are bad and to be avoided as far as possible. The most important thing, however, that sickness has in common with other temptations is that they all have to do with the conflict between the kingdom of God and the kingdom of Satan. It is significant that the prayer before the sacramental anointing of the sick begins, "May all the devil's power over you be brought to nothing by the laying on of our hands . . ." The notion that sickness has to do with the power of the devil, that the patient is somehow in the power of Satan, is one that would be rejected out of hand by almost any civilized man today. It seems to belong to an age before medicine became a science, when men made do with charms and incantations because they had nothing more reliable to use. It seems akin to primitive belief that every sick man is under a spell or bewitched by an enemy. I hope to be able to show, nevertheless, that it is an integral part of the teaching of the New Testament and that it is not such obvious nonsense as at first it seems.

In the first place, although there can be no doubt at all that the Evangelists and Christ himself talk as though physical sickness and the power of Satan were closely linked, this will not of itself suffice to show that the belief is a part of what the New Testament teaches. Thus, for example, Christ certainly talks as though David were the author of Psalms 110 (Matt. 22.43.), but we do not claim that this view is a part of Christ's teaching. If we hold that the psalm is Davidic, our opinion is a matter of human investigation, not of divine faith. In general, most Christians would say that it was no part of Christ's mission to correct points of biblical scholarship or to change the received opinions of his time in peripheral matters. Now, it might be thought that in treating sickness as a manifestation of Satan's power, Christ and the Evangelists were simply falling in with the accepted opinions of the time. In order to decide such a question we have to ask whether the matter is something peripheral or whether it is central to Christ's teaching. This is, of course, by no means a simple question. In the last analysis only the voice of the whole Christian community can say definitively what is central to the Christian faith, and certainly it is a task in which the theologian must help the exegete.

One way to begin answering the question in our case would be to see what would happen to the Gospels if we treated all the passages about casting out devils as metaphorical ways of referring to cures; would the central story be affected? It seems to me that it would be hopelessly distorted. The encounters with the devils which Christ has in his cures are part of the story of his defeat of Satan which is essential to the Gospel message.

To remove the Satan element would be to take away their point in the story.

It is hardly necessary to substantiate here in detail the first point, that in the Gospels cure of sickness and casting out of devils are closely linked. It is not that they were identified, on the contrary they were often distinguished: "all those suffering from various diseases were brought to him, whether they were racked by pain, or possessed by demons, or epileptic or paralysed. And he cured them." (Matt. 4.24.) But the cure of possession and of disease are regarded as the same sort of activity. Both were defeats for Satan. In Luke, the woman who for eighteen years had been bent double and unable to raise her head is described by Christ as "this daughter of Abraham whom Satan has bound". (13.16.) Demonic possession, sin and sickness are, of course, three quite different things, particularly from the moral point of view, but for the New Testament they are linked together by their common connection with the "prince of this world". The story in Matthew 9 about the paralytic helps to make plain the connection between them. Here the cure of the sick man is a manifestation of defeat of sin: "That you may know that the Son of Man has power on earth to forgive sins . . ." Christ's summary of his mission in his cryptic message to "that fox Herod" pinpoints exactly the function of the cures in his life: "I am driving out demons and performing cures today and tomorrow; it is on the third day that I reach my goal." (Luke 13.32.)

The cures are preliminary skirmishes with Satan's ministers before the final confrontation. From this point of view the saying of Jesus in Mark 3.24–29 is of great interest. When he is accused of casting out demons by the power of Beelzebub the archdemon, he claims to be "entering the castle of the mighty lord" to imprison him and to plunder his possessions. His power over the demons is a sign that the end of the reign of Satan is at hand. In Matthew's version the point is made even more explicitly: "If by the Spirit of God I cast out demons, then evidently the kingdom of God has now made its way to you." (12.28.) Luke adds a final elegant touch; he has changed "Spirit of God" to "finger of God" (11.20), in reminiscence of the Egyptian magicians who, defeated by Moses' superior power, said to Pharaoh, "The finger of God is here." Just as the miracles of Moses were signs that the liberation of the Hebrews was imminent, so the miraculous cures of Christ were anticipations of his final victory.

"The Father . . . has rescued us from the power of darkness and transferred us into the kingdom of his beloved Son." (Col. 1.13.) I want to suggest that sickness has somewhat the same relation to the realm of darkness that the sacraments have to the kingdom of the Son. Human infirmity, everything which tends of itself to degrade mankind, is a sign of the power of Satan, as the sacraments are signs of the power of Christ. The parallel must not be pressed too closely, for, of course, the sacraments of Christ bring about what they signify, they realize the saving power of Christ; the same cannot be said of the symbols of Satan's kingdom. Perhaps a closer analogy is to be found in the notion of "sacramentals" than of sacraments proper, though in the case of the phenomenon of "possession" the New Testament suggests a "real presence" of the demons. It may be necessary at this point to deal with the objection that sickness does not necessarily degrade a man, that in fact a truer dignity may be shown by a man wrestling patiently with some infirmity of body or mind than by a complacent young man proud of his "fitness". This is of course true, but the point is that a man only shows dignity in dealing with his sickness precisely because it is his enemy; its tendency is to degrade him and it is by overcoming this that he shows forth his humanity. Satan's power is devoted to the degradation of man, and his unhappiness, but there is a scale of values in this matter. The most important thing for Satan is that man should be finally unhappy, that he should be cheated of his ultimate goal; in order to achieve this it may be expedient to permit him a relative and temporary happiness in this world. The wicked may have to be allowed to flourish like the green bay tree as a means to ultimate sterility, but such flourishing is not characteristic of the work of Satan. Of itself the influence of Satan appears not in pleasure and vitality and joy of any kind, but in misery and boredom and pain. These things show us what the kingdom of evil is like, just as the sacraments show us what the kingdom of Christ is like.

But I have said more than this. It is not only that sickness shows us what Satan's power is like, I have also claimed that it is due to him. I do not mean by this to produce an alternative to the germ theory of disease. I do not mean that sickness is brought about by the devil and *not* by the causes isolated by medical science. What I mean is that the fact that man is subject to disease is a result of his domination by the power of evil. It is because man deliberately placed himself under this power that he is liable to bodily infirmities; if he had not fallen he would have been preserved from such evils. Thus sickness shows forth the realm of Satan and every cure, quite apart from whether it works a moral improvement in the individual who is cured, represents a setback for that realm.

It is for this reason that the power to cure and to cast out devils is an integral part of the Christian work: "He then called to him his twelve apostles and gave them authority over unclean spirits and power to drive them out, and power to heal any disease or infirmity. The names of the twelve are . . ." (Matt. 10.1–2.) In his instructions to the Twelve he says: "As you go along proclaim that the Kingdom of Heaven is at hand. Heal the sick, raise the dead, make lepers clean, and drive out demons." (10.7–8.) Mark's account of the mission of the Twelve contains a detail omitted in Matthew: "Accordingly they set out and exhorted the people to a change of heart; they also drove out many demons and cured many who were sick *by anointing them with oil.*" (6.12–13; Gospel for the Mass of the Chrism.)

The ceremony of anointing is, as we have seen, throughout the Old Testament associated with the presence of the Spirit of God. By the anointing the power of the evil spirit is replaced by that of the Holy Spirit, the Spirit of Christ. It will be remembered that a similar anointing is associated during the baptismal ceremonies with the rejection of Satan and the acceptance of Christ.

The power which Christ's missionaries exercise over demons is associated in Luke's account with Christ's definitive victory over Satan. "The seventy-two returned in high spirits. 'Master', they said, 'even the demons are subject to us in your name.' 'Yes,' he said to them, 'I saw Satan fall from heaven like lightning.'" (10.17–18.) The accuser of mankind has lost his power and is to be replaced by the Advocate, the Paraclete who pleads for mankind before God. The victory of Christ is described in the same terms in the Apocalypse:

> That huge dragon, the ancient serpent, was hurled down,
> He who is called the devil and Satan, He who leads the
> whole world astray. He was hurled down to earth, and his
>   angels were hurled down with him,
> And I heard a voice crying in heaven: Now has our God
>   brought victory and power and royalty
> And his Christ has authority
> For the Accuser of our brethren has been   hurled down,
> He who accused them before our God day and night . . .
> Woe to you earth and sea,
> For the devil has gone down to you in great wrath
> Knowing that his days are numbered.
>
> [Ap. 12.9–12.]

This passage may help us to answer the question: If sickness is the work of Satan and Satan has been defeated, how is it that there is still sickness in the world? Satan has been radically defeated, the damnation of mankind has been averted and in Christ man is offered divine life, but the sacramentals of Satan's kingdom survive, the victory of Christ is not yet physically visible, the divine life within us does not yet appear in our bodies and will not do so until the resurrection. In heaven the power of the Accuser is broken but he has been cast down to earth and on earth his power still survives, although his days are numbered. In the meantime it is part of the Christian mission to wage war against his power on earth; the Christian ministry of healing is a part of this war. The victory of Christ has not meant the sudden and total abolition either of sin or of sickness and human misery; he has left his Church to carry on his work. There is, however, an important difference between the Church's mission of sanctification and of healing. The divine life which Christ brings to us through the sacraments of the Church is identical with the life we shall share after the resurrection. From the point of view of sanctification, the charity we now have "will abide", we are already in heaven. But the healing of our bodies which the Church may bring is not identical with the health which we shall have after the resurrection. Our present bodily health is only a sign of the bodily glory which is to come, it is not continuous with it. It can, however, be a sacramental sign of that glory, and this I believe is what is involved in the anointing of the sick.

When we speak of the healing mission of the Church, there are, it seems to me, at least four things to be distinguished: miracles, charismatic healing, sacramental anointing and the progress of medicine. The last of these I offer merely as a subject for investigation; I think it might be worth asking whether there is a significant connection between the Christian tradition of care for the sick, of the sacredness of the body, of concern for the helpless and of opposition to substitutes for healing such as magic, infanticide and euthanasia, and the growth of medical science in Western Europe. I am not of course suggesting that a man is a better doctor for being a Christian, but rather that a society formed in the Christian tradition may have been a more congenial context for the development of medicine than non-Christian societies. This is, however, at the moment, mere speculation.

Charismatic healing seems to have been a fairly normal feature of life in the early Church; prayer and the laying on of hands brought strength and health to the sick. There is no reason to suppose that these cures would be accepted as "miracles" according to the stringent criteria adopted, say, at Lourdes. For that matter, a very large number of people who return cured from Lourdes are not regarded as the subjects of miraculous intervention. A miracle in this sense would be a dramatic cure which simply could not be explained in terms of any natural cause, it must not be merely the hastening of a recovery which might have come anyway or a cure which might be due to psychological causes or good luck. Very little is known (and hardly any of it by the present author) about the effects of psychological conditions upon health, but it would be taking no great risk to claim that generally speaking a patient will do better if he feels himself surrounded by loving friends who care for him, than if he is alone, a stranger in a hostile environment. Hysterical conditions and neurotic states can complicate recovery from the most "objective" ailments. Rapid cures which are due to the alleviation of these would not normally be counted miraculous—the doctor is pleased and perhaps surprised but he is not astounded. It is reasonable to think that most charismatic healing is of this kind. To bring to the patient a sense of the presence of Christ and of his fellow Christians, to strengthen his faith and his awareness of the love by which he is surrounded, to restore to him a sense of belonging to a community in which his life matters; all these things might be expected to help his recovery. This is not an attempt to "explain away" charismatic healing in "natural" terms. The sense of community available to Christians is not something natural.

Unity in charity is not, indeed, identical with an experience of fellowship, but a specific Christian experience of love may be expected normally to flow from it. If we say that the Eucharist properly celebrated will normally foster an experience of community we are not "explaining away" the Lord's Supper; if we say that an adult baptized at the Easter Vigil will normally experience at many levels of consciousness a renewal of life, a "rebirth", this is not to "explain away" baptism. When we say that Eucharist or baptism is sacramental we mean that they have a reality at a depth beyond this experience, so that it even makes sense to baptize infants, it even makes sense to celebrate the Eucharist alone or amongst an uncomprehending and inactive congregation. Of course for centuries our sacramental theology, hag-ridden by anti-Protestantism, has concentrated on the non-experiential aspect of the sacraments almost to the point of treating them as magic rites; it is as though, having insisted that a man can be a human being even when deprived of arms and legs, we went on to treat these limbs as optional extras.

Now I would suggest that when we speak of the anointing of the sick as sacramental we are claiming that we have here a reality of healing which goes beyond the experience of belonging ordinarily associated with charismatic healing (so that, for example, it even makes sense to anoint an unconscious man). The effect which might ordinarily be produced by the *experience* of union in love with the rest of the Church is here brought about *sacramentally*. "Give him back to your holy Church . . ." In the sacrament the community draws the sick man back to life in the community. The will to live, the emotional need to be physically with his friends (which will ordinarily assist his recovery) is, I suggest, the sacramental reality which represents and brings about the reality of grace, the desire for community in charity, "eucharistic by desire". If this view is correct there was something peculiarly bizarre about the custom, now happily being abandoned, of anointing a dying man after he has received Viaticum. Anointing is ordered towards the Eucharist, not towards death. The Viaticum, the genuine "last sacrament", is the Eucharist as ordered towards death and resurrection, the last sacramental Communion before sharing the heavenly banquet.

The Epistle for the Mass of the Chrism is part of the passage from St. James which is normally quoted as the authority for the existence of a sacrament of anointing in the early Church. The Apostle is winding up his message with remarks about the Christian life in various situations: "If anyone among you is suffering, let him pray; if anyone is joyful, let him sing a canticle. If anyone among you is sick let him call in the elders [presbyters: priests] of the Church and let them pray over him after anointing him with oil in the name of the Lord. The prayer of faith will save the sick man and the Lord will raise him up. If he has committed sins they will be forgiven. Confess then your sins one to another, and pray one for another, so that you may be healed." (Jas. 5.13–16.) We have the authority of the Council of Trent for saying, what seems obvious, that we have here not merely a matter of ordinary prayer for the sick, but an actual sacramental ceremony. Notice in particular the constant reference to the community; it is one "among you" who is sick, it is the whole official Church, represented by the "presbyters", who come to visit him. The most natural interpretation of the reference to forgiveness of sins is that the sickness might be regarded as a punishment for his sin (not necessarily, of course "*if* he has committed sins") and the healing would be a manifestation of the fact that he is forgiven. Compare: "That you may know that the Son of Man has power on earth to forgive sins . . ." The picture we have is one of the whole community wielding the power of Christ's pity and love on behalf of one of its suffering members.

It is impossible to end without some comment on the present pastoral practice of this sacrament. If our view of it is correct the ceremony should essentially be, and appear to be, a matter of inviting the sick man back to his place in the worshipping community. The representatives of the parish come to him to say that he has been missed from the assembly and to pray that he will come back to them. Now in our present practice extreme unction is not a summoning back to life, it is a death sentence. Relatives fear to "call in the priest" because of the effect it may have on the sick man, for it is generally recognized that there is not much hope of recovery when this happens. "He has been anointed" is an indication, in Catholic circles, that he is on his deathbed. The thing is a vicious spiral; because the priest is not called in except as a last resort, anointing is left to a moment at which only a miracle could save the patient. We have no right to expect miracles of sacraments. The general healing effect of which we have spoken, the restoration of the will to live, will not ordinarily save a man on his deathbed. From this results the popular belief that this sacrament is not normally a healing rite but a preparation for death. The first reform we need, therefore, is a much earlier administration and a rooting out of the idea that anointing means that we have given up all hope. According to the Council of Trent this sacrament is for those who are seriously ill or near to death; it must not be trivialized, it is not for colds and headaches. We could well see the words of the council as an expression of the idea that a Christian ought not to be hypochondriac, he ought not to trouble the community with his minor ailments. But when he suffers from something serious, something from which he could die, then he can call on the resources of healing love in his fellow Christians. The insistence of the council on the seriousness of the illness is in fact intended as a corrective of an abuse which grew up through too great a "spiritualization" of the sacrament. Some of those (particularly in the East) who thought that the sacrament could not be directed towards the good of the body argued that since it was for the healing of ailments of the soul and since the soul was liable to sin at any time, the sacrament should be administered as frequently as possible. The Fathers of Trent, in combating this trivialization, swung the Church in the opposite direction, with the result that we have in practice used anointing as a sacrament of death.

Finally, just as our consideration of the Eucharist led to the idea that the Christian community cannot just express itself sacramentally in Church, so we must conclude that Christian concern for sickness cannot be expressed merely sacramentally in the anointing of the sick. Just as the Mass should be the expression and the centre of a social solidarity in the parish, so the anointing of the sick should be the culmination of the parishioners' concern for each other in sickness. It is true that a visit from certain parishioners, particularly the more "active", may sometimes result in a relapse rather than a recovery on the part of a sensitive patient, but this is a comment on the situation in which we have allowed communal parish life to fall into the hands of the organizers and the committee-minded. The coming of the priest (and why only one?—St. James does after all explicitly suggest that it should be a matter of them all, not just the man "on sick calls") should be the final sacramental expression of the interest shown by the whole community in "one among you who is sick".

7

SEX AND THE SACRED

I<small>N</small> order to talk theologically about sex, we have to look at
the place which sex has in the divine plan, in the revelation of God. It might be imagined that we could explain
what God has revealed to us about sex, so that we could compare or contrast it with what Freud or D. H. Lawrence or
Dr. Kinsey has to say about sex. But this would not be quite
accurate; what we want to discover is not what God says about
sex, but what sex as interpreted by the Old Testament, by
Christ and by the sacraments, has to show us about God.

We may begin with a poem which has been inserted at the
very beginning of the Bible. Its opening lines give us the theme
of the poem: "In the beginning God created the heavens and
the earth." It is to be a poem about what creation means. God
is represented as working, as a good Hebrew should, for six
days and resting on the seventh. This is not, of course, because
the author thought of God as subject to the Hebrew law, for
he is the author of that law; but he wanted to make the point
that human life, when it stays true to itself by following the
law of God, is a representation of, a showing forth of, God's
activity.

> The earth was without form and void, and darkness was
> upon the face of the deep. And the Spirit of God was mov-
> ing over the face of the waters.

As a prologue we are shown the creative Spirit of God, the
breath of God which inspired the heroes and great men of
Israel, brooding or hovering over the dark waters to make
them fertile. Later, after the coming of Light, the waters are to
be divided as the waters of the Red Sea were divided at the

creation of the Hebrew people. The image is closely related to the Babylonian myth in which mankind is brought forth after the god has conquered and slit open the dragon of the waters.[1] Conquest and fertilization are very closely linked ideas. The plough subdues the earth, conquers it, divides it, and makes it fertile. This remote hint of sexuality at the beginning of the poem prepares the way for a later point. During the ensuing days God prepares the framework of the world, the stage upon which man is to act. On the fifth day he makes animal life, and here a significant change takes place. Hitherto God has simply spoken and things have happened: "God said: let there be light . . . Let there be a vault in the midst of the waters . . ." and so on. Now for the first time he speaks directly to his creatures. Having made the animals, "God blessed them, saying, 'Be fruitful and multiply and fill the waters in the seas, and let birds multiply on the earth.'"

The suggestion conveyed here is that these higher creatures are in some sense on speaking terms with God; he can speak to them, because in some remote way they are like him, they too give life. They increase and multiply and reflect his great work of creation. The giving of new life, bringing a new living thing into being, is the best image we have of creation. It is not creation, of course, because it takes place as part of a complex causal system, whereas creation starts from nowhere and nothing, but it represents creation to us.

On the final day man is created and with him the resemblance to the Creator is no longer merely hinted at, it is explicitly stated:

> Let us make, man in our own image, after our likeness, and let them have dominion over the fish of the sea and the birds of the air and the cattle and over all the earth. So God created man in his own image, in the image of God he created

---

[1] See Chapter 1.

him: male and female he created them. And God blessed
them, and said to them, "Be fruitful and multiply and fill
the earth and subdue it, and have dominion . . ."

It is insistently stressed that man is the image of God and this
is associated with two functions. Man is to have dominion
over the world, and he is to increase and multiply. In these he
mirrors the creative and ruling power of God.

From the beginning God made man male and female. The
first thing that is said about man after he has been given the
mission of ruling the world is that he is the father of a family,
or rather the father and mother of a family. From the beginning
God made man and woman. The author insists on this because
some of his contemporaries regarded women as a kind of over-
sight, not intended by God in creation; women were beings
who had not succeeded in being men.

From the beginning, therefore, the Scriptures make of
human sexuality something associated with the image of God
in man. This is by no means the whole story, but it is the
beginning of the story. I have said that the production of new
life is the best image we have of creation, but in the production
of new human life we have more than an image of creation,
we have creation itself. At the very centre of his being man
does not depend on any other creatures, but on God alone.
This is the root of his freedom and his transcendent dignity,
and this is why he alone amongst material things can enter into
himself to find God. Other things are simply parts of the world
and find their perfection simply in playing their parts in the
world, but in the end man's perfection is in himself. No human
being owes his deepest self to any other creature; each human
life is a unique creation of God. Thus while in other animals
new life is the image of creation, in human animals there is
not only the image but the reality of creation. The womb of
the mother is the scene of a direct and special intervention of
God himself. This is the first reason why we believe human

sexuality to be especially sacred. There are other and greater reasons still.

The poem we have been considering in the first chapter of Genesis is immediately followed by another story of creation, and here once more the emphasis is on creation as the production of new life. In this story the image is the new life which comes suddenly to the desert at the beginning of the rains. First we see the dry parched desert:

> No plant of the field was yet in the earth and no herb of the field had yet sprung up—for the Lord God had not caused it to rain upon the earth, and there was no man to till the ground.

Then a spring of water appeared in the waste-land and "watered the whole face of the ground". Instantly life begins. The Lord models a man out of clay and breathes into him the breath of life, so that he comes alive, living by the breath of God himself.

This story emphasizes, even more explicitly than the other, that man, because he lives by God's spirit, is the centre of creation; all the rest is made for him. The Lord first of all plants a garden for the man and then he says: "It is not good that the man should be alone; I will make him a helper fit for him." First of all the Lord tries the other animals: "He formed every beast of the field and every bird of the air and brought them to the man . . ." The man gives them their names, organizes them, gives them their jobs in the world. But, the story goes on, this was all right in its way but it was not enough. "But for the man there was not found a helper fit for him." The other animals are merely subject to man, they obey him, he rules them and for this very reason they are not enough; they are simply made of the dust of the earth without the breath of God in them.

Finally the Lord makes woman from the body of man himself, and the man sings:

This at last is bone of my bones
and flesh of my flesh
she shall be called Woman
because she was taken out of Man.

"Therefore", the author goes on, "a man leaves his father and mother and cleaves to his wife, and they become one flesh. And the man and his wife were both naked, and were not ashamed."

This last phrase prepares the way for the story that is to follow. So far all is order and clarity. There is a simple hierarchy. First is God, then his creature man living by the breath of God. Next is man's helper, the woman who is made from man himself, so much so that when they are united sexually they become as it were one body. Below woman come the beasts of the field. Everything is idyllic and smoothly organized, there are no agonizing choices, it is a protected world such as we only glimpse for rare moments in the nursery, even the animals are all Peter Rabbit and his friends. It is a charming world and completely unlike the one we live in, though we are constantly tempted to think that with a few extra adjustments our world could be like that. In fact we have a higher task than that of returning to the nursery.

This idyllic world is destroyed by disobedience. The author represents the destruction as an inversion of the hierarchy of the world. Whereas the established order was God, man, woman, beast, now it is the beast, the serpent, who persuades the woman, the woman who persuades the man, and the man who disobeys God. The "natural order" has been overturned and there is a partial return to chaos. In consequence of the breaking of friendship with God disorder appears in human life, elements which ought to be working smoothly together to form an interlocking pattern now work against each other. It is as though some complex piece of machinery has been dropped on the floor; all the separate little bits are still buzzing away doing their own jobs but these jobs no longer automatically mesh with the functioning of the other bits. Before the Fall it was enough for each element in the pattern to look after its own perfection, and it could be taken for granted that this would contribute towards the good of the whole, but now this is no longer true. It is no longer enough for things to be good in themselves—their relationship to other things has got twisted. There is conflict now not just between good and evil, but between good and good. The woman will desire her husband and yet this will involve the pains of childbirth; the thorns and thistles, which like "every plant yielding seed according to its kind", are good and were made for man, now battle against him in his work.

So the author of this story sees flowing from the Fall all the hostilities and fears of the world. The hostility of the animals— "I will put enmity between you and the woman"—the hostility of all nature, the paradoxes and conflicts of sex, the drudgery of work, the new fears and shame that are associated with sex, and finally the fear of death itself, for the breath of life is withdrawn from man and he returns in a short time to dust.

These early tales from Genesis map out the complex place which human sexuality is to have in the divine plan. In the first place sexuality is a blessing from God. Through it man imitates God in creation, in it he reaches a special kind of personal fulfilment, man and woman become two in one flesh. Through the Fall, however, it has become a locus of conflict and tragedy. It is significant that the animal chosen to persuade the woman is the serpent, which in Middle-Eastern mythology is the symbol of autonomous sexuality, sexuality operating in isolation from a total human context, sexuality going quietly mad by itself.

The balance of optimism and realism contained in these stories is to be characteristic of the place of sex in divine revelation. Without revelation we usually tend to oversimplify life; there is a strong pressure on men who rely simply upon their human experience to either a fundamental pessimism—sex is at best a necessary evil, the wise man will avoid it if he can—or an unreal optimism which supposes that when you have said that it is good and glorious you have said all that you need to say. These positions express moods or experiences which any adult might have at some particular time, but our faith reminds us of other factors which we must take account of even though they are not obvious to us at the moment.

The isolation of sex from its total human context, which is a result of the Fall, is linked very closely with the isolation of the individual from his total communal context. Nothing is more revealing of the false position in which we can so easily place sex than the uncritical use of phrases like "sexual hunger", "sex-starved", "sexual appetite"; these phrases have a perfectly good meaning, but they suggest that sex is an appetite alongside and similar to the appetite for food and drink. This can be very confusing indeed and results from thinking of man outside his true racial context. As a matter of biology the individual needs to eat sometimes or he will go out of existence; he does not need to eat all the time, but sometimes. Eating is therefore a biological necessity for the individual. Sexual activity, on the other hand, is a biological necessity for the race. If the human race does not have sexual activity in some individuals it will go out of existence; there does not need to be sexual activity in all individuals but there has to be in some. As a matter of sheer biology sex belongs not to the individual as such but to the individual in his relation to the whole human race. If we try to consider man in isolation from this context we shall also consider his sexuality in isolation from the rest of his life, and this is where all the mistakes are waiting to be made.

The fall of man is presented in Genesis as being due to man's attempt to be in absolute control of his own life. "You shall be as gods", says the serpent. The rest of the Bible is concerned with the story of the return of man to God and in this story the theme of sexual love has an extremely important part to play. The story opens with Abraham; he is the beginning of salvation, and the essential thing about Abraham is that he has faith. Faith is the very opposite of the first sin. Adam sought to be independent of God; faith, on the other hand, means recognition of our own inadequacy, a total, unconditional dependence upon God. Abraham, as he is presented in the Bible, both in Genesis and in St. Paul's epistles, is the primordial man of faith—but what was the particular *topic* of his faith? It was this: that his wife Sarah, who was manifestly past the age of childbearing, would have a child. It was through this child and his descendants that the plan of God was to be realized; through him Abraham was to be the father of many nations, through him the world was to be saved once more. But humanly speaking it was impossible that there should be any such child. Nevertheless Abraham believed God, he believed that the barren woman would become fertile by the power of God though this was impossible to human nature. And this is the primordial Hebrew picture of grace. The intervention of God to do what man by his own nature cannot do was seen in concrete terms as a supernatural fertility. There are other such stories in the earlier books of the Old Testament and always their purpose is the same; the hero who is to save his people is born "not of blood, nor of the will of the flesh, nor of man's will, but of God". The effect of grace is new life in the desert, fruitfulness where there was barrenness.

After the establishment of the kingdom in the Promised Land we no longer get stories of the barren woman giving birth but in its place we have the recurring theme of the "Virgin Israel". The point of this image is the same as that of the barren woman. Israel is a virgin dedicated to marriage with Yahweh alone. She is not to look for human aid, she is not to make dubious political alliances with the neighbouring pagan states, she is to reserve herself for her marriage with Yahweh. It is Yahweh, and not any human power, who will make her fertile. The poems of Jeremiah are haunted by a nostalgia for the betrothal of Israel and Yahweh which took place in the

desert at the time of the first Pasch. Notice that this new creation, the creation of Israel, comes from the waste-land:

> I remember the devotion of your youth,
> your love as a bride,
> How you followed me in the wilderness,
> in a land not sown.
> Israel was holy to the Lord,
> The first-fruits of his harvest. [Jer. 2.2–3.]

Notice the juxtaposition of the desert, the land not sown, and
the new life: the first-fruits of his harvest.

And in that day, says Yahweh, you will call me "my husband" and no longer will you call me "my Lord". (Hos. 2.16.)

Many of the Old-Testament poems refer immediately to the
contemporary political and religious situations, but they are
prophetic poems in that they look beyond the present to the
destiny of Israel in God's plan. However dimly the Hebrews
themselves may have realized this, Israel had in fact a mission
to the whole world which went beyond political terms. To say
that the Old Testament is the word of God is to say that what
speaks of the destiny of Israel speaks of her destiny in the plan
of God, and the destiny of Israel in Christ. With the prophets
who wrote when the Hebrews were in exile the image of the
Virgin Israel takes on a new application. For them the restoration of Israel is seen as the marriage which the virgin is await-
ing. A poem in the Book of Isaiah says:

> You shall no more be termed Forsaken,
> and your land shall no more be termed Desolate;
> But you shall be called "My delight in her"
> and your land shall be called "Married".
> . . . and as the bridegroom rejoices over the bride
> so shall your God rejoice over you. [Isa. 62.4–5.]

What is looked forward to, then, is a new marriage between
Israel and Yahweh. Sometimes the Messiah is seen as the fruit

of the supernatural fertility of this union; as in the famous passage in Isaiah, "Behold a virgin shall conceive and bear a son, and you shall call his name 'God with us'", or, again, the picture of the Servant as a plant growing out of barren ground. Sometimes, on the other hand, the messianic king, as in Psalm 44, is seen as the husband and Israel as the bride. Each of these themes is taken up and fulfilled in the New Testament.

The restoration of Israel, the fulfilment of her destiny, was seen as the marriage of the Virgin Israel with Yahweh; the messianic age was to be the marriage feast, the sacred meal associated with the marriage of Israel and God. This is the background to the story of the virgin birth of Christ in St. Matthew and St. Luke. The Virgin Mary represents and sums up the Virgin Israel; in her the prophecies are fulfilled.

The Holy Spirit shall come upon thee, and the Power of the Most High shall overshadow thee. Therefore the Holy One that will be born of thee shall be called the Son of God.

Mary is the bride of Yahweh who brings forth salvation without the power of man. In her the mission of Israel to bring together mankind and God is brought to fulfilment.

We should completely misunderstand the significance of Mary's virginity in the divine plan if we thought of it in terms of sterility. The whole point of it is that it involves a divine fertility, a marriage with God. It would also be a mistake to see her virginity as we can and do see the virginity of others, as only a renunciation, a form of asceticism. Renunciation belongs to the interim period between Christ's first and second coming. Mary's perpetual virginity is not a renunciation but the eschatological fulfilment of sexuality such as the just will enjoy after the resurrection. In his own birth Christ, then, is seen as the hero born of the marriage of Yahweh with the virgin Israel, but he is also more commonly seen as the bridegroom and the new Israel as his bride. One of the first messianic titles he takes to himself is that of the bridegroom. He is asked why it is that the disciples of John and the Pharisees fast, while his disciples do not. He says, "Do the companions of the bridegroom fast while the bridegroom is with them?" He is the bridegroom and his presence is the messianic feast. St. Mark follows this immediately with the story of the disciples plucking ears of wheat on the sabbath—another image of the sacred nuptial meal. In St. John's Gospel Christ's first sign takes place in the context of the marriage feast and Christ himself constantly compares his coming to a royal wedding feast, e.g., in the parables of the wedding feast, the wise and foolish virgins, the king's son. As Messiah he is the bridegroom come to wed the faithful, the Church. As the Apocalypse puts it:

> One of the seven angels said: Come and I will show you the bride, the wife of the lamb. And he took me up in spirit to a great and high mountain and showed me the holy city, Jerusalem, coming down out of heaven from God. [Apoc. 21.9–10.]

In Genesis we have seen marriage as a reflection, an image of divine creativeness, and in these later passages we see how it is used by God as an image of his redemptive love for mankind. We find this theme explicitly developed in its final form in the famous passage in the Epistle to the Ephesians (5.25–32).

> Husbands, love your wives as Christ loved the Church.
> He delivered himself up for her.

All human love must involve a sacrifice of oneself, and in Christian marriage this sacrifice is sacramentally united to Christ's sacrifice by which he delivered himself up for the Church.

We may ask what it is about the love of husband and wife that makes it so suitable an image of the love of Christ for his Church, or which made it such a suitable image of the love of Yahweh for Israel. In the first place, it is a total and unconditional love, which does not hold anything back. It is a sacrificial love, a giving of oneself. The love of man and wife is not always of this kind, but this is how marriage is to be in the revelation of God and by entering into the revelation of God this is what marriage can become. For the revelation of God is not just information; it does not, for example, simply tell us what an ideal marriage ought to be like—this would be very cold comfort. Revelation is a life which we lead, a world in which we live. It is a new creation which we enter in entering the sacramental life of the Church. Being married, for the Christian, means sharing the sacramental life in a special way.

In the second place, marriage makes a suitable image of the love of Christ for his Church because it is a union; the Church is the body of Christ as the wife's body is her husband's. The wife does not belong to the husband as something he owns, any more than his own body does; she belongs to him as his body, and the same of course is true of the husband—he belongs in this way to his wife. The husband can say of his wife, not "This belongs to me", not "This body is mine", but "This is my body", for they are two in one flesh. And this is what Christ says of his Church. Over the bread and wine which, as offerings of the Church, symbolize the Church itself offered to the Father, he says, "This is my body." This does not mean that the Church and Christ are one person, any more than husband and wife become one person. The union of marriage in the Kingdom of God is no threat to the personal integrity of each partner. On the contrary, the personality of each is reaffirmed by his gift of himself to the other. But they are two who share a common life as Christ and the Church share a common life which is the Spirit of God, divine love.

What I have been trying to do is to show the place which sex and marriage have in the divine plan as means by which God is revealed to us. This is only half of the subject and less than half of what the Scriptures have to say about the topic. We also have to consider sex in relation to our attainment of God, to locate sexual love in the broader context of the divine life of love in us. We have in fact to consider the *moral* theology of sex. By recognizing marriage as one of the sacraments of Christ, Christianity asserts both that it shows us Christ and that it is a way of being incorporated in him. Sexual love is thus an opportunity for sanctity, but since every such opportunity can be the occasion of failure we must also be concerned with the ways in which sex and marriage are affected by the disorders consequent upon the Fall, and in particular with the dehumanizing of sex by which it loses touch with the rest of human life and carries on an autonomous life of its own.

Sex for the Christian is sacred in a quite technical sense, it is something which contains and shows forth the creative power of God, and sex in marriage is more sacred still since it contains and shows forth the redeeming love of God. But to be sacred means first of all to be dangerous. It can mean much more, but it first means this: "No man can look upon God and live." If we profane the sacred we shall be destroyed by it. This is the inner meaning of the taboos with which sex is surrounded; they are expressions, or began as expressions, of the reverence and fear which is proper in the presence of something sacred. Of course other people's taboos always look ridiculous and in a rapidly changing world, the last generation but one is already "other people", their taboos are foreign to us and are apt to look absurd. This does not matter—it is not the nature of the taboo that counts—but there would be, I think, something seriously wrong with a society which did not have any taboos about sex. It is not dangerous because it is bad, it is dangerous because it is sacred, powerful, capable if it is divorced from the world of love of destroying the personality as effectively as a drug, and equally capable of bringing us, through the power of Christ's passion, to eternal union with God.

8

THE SACRAMENT OF MARRIAGE

I WANT to begin with a picture I do not accept, and I will try to explain why I do not accept it and what I want to put in its place. It goes like this—"Sex is first of all a matter of fulfilment . . . it is an appetite which must be satisfied one way or another; sexual desire is something implanted in us by Nature and Nature's purpose is the maintenance of the race. But Nature, with her usual lavish hand, has given us far more sexual desire than is really necessary, just as she makes far more cod's eggs than are really necessary to keep up the population of cod. Because our sexual desires are stronger and more frequent than is really necessary we are led into various kinds of competition and violence, disorder and war. In order to regulate this situation man has invented the institution of marriage. Marriage is rather like the institution of private property, to which indeed it is closely related. Men have an appetite for possessions greater than is really necessary, and to regulate this appetite we grow hedges round bits of land and say to a man 'Go in there and own away to your heart's content but don't come over the hedge into my land.' Private property means that a man may perhaps have *less* than he would like, but what he has is *secure*." Marriage, according to this picture is a fence around the sexual appetite just as the hedge is a fence around the appetite for possessions. Marriage is a limit set on sexual activity for the sake of other people.

I do not accept this picture. There are a whole lot of things about it that seem wrong to me. I notice, for example, that it betrays a deep hostility to sex. In this picture sex is a dangerous animal which has to be caged by marriage; there is no positive value in it except that it is the fulfilment of an appetite, it provides a satisfaction which we are expected to feel guilty about outside marriage and not guilty about inside marriage. Our minds are not constructed to work these kinds of tricks, so if we have this picture we just feel fairly guilty about sex anyway; the only difference is that outside marriage we think we have a *reason* for feeling guilty.

According to this picture marriage is something external to sex: there is no necessary connection between them except the one supplied by the needs of society. Marriage is two things, sex plus certain limits; sex outside marriage is just the one thing.

Now will this theory stand up to critical examination? Let us just reflect for a moment on the analogy with hedges and property. According to this theory there is something called an appetite for property which is kept within limits by the hedges. When it is satisfied inside the hedges it is OK, when it is satisfied outside the hedges it is not OK. Legitimate ownership is two things, satisfying an appetite for property *plus* limits, "property is legalized robbery"; robbery is just the one thing satisfying an appetite for property. But once you begin to examine this story it falls to pieces. Take another look at this appetite for property. How can you have an appetite for property if there is no ownership? Supposing there were no hedges, there would be no property and so you could not have an appetite for it. What would *count* as satisfying your appetite? There is in fact no such thing as a basic datum called the appetite for property which has to be regulated by ownership; on the contrary there is a basic datum called ownership and the appetite for this may outstep its proper limits and become an appetite for robbery. An owner is not a robber plus title deeds; a robber is someone pretending to be an owner although he has no title deeds. An owner is not a robber and then something more, a robber is a defective owner.

Now I think we can have the same destructive thoughts about the picture of sex that we have been given. Just as the

urge to possess depends for its meaning on the institution
of legitimate ownership, so the human sexual desire depends
for its meaning on the institution of marriage. And just as robbery is imitation ownership and would be meaningless without
ownership, so sex without marriage is just imitation marriage.
It is defective marriage, something is lacking to it.

The two cases of ownership and marriage are, I think, parallel, but they are not on the same plane. For one thing, you can
and apparently do have societies in which there is no institution of private property, and it follows not as a sociological or
as a psychological fact but as a *logical* consequence that there
is no robbery and no desire for robbery. On the other hand,
there are no human societies in which there is not the institution of marriage, though it takes different forms in different
societies.

All this is really to say that what is wrong with the picture
we have been examining is that it has missed out any mention
of love. In human beings sexual desire cannot be dissociated
from the desire to love and be loved. The connection is not
always simple; the relevance of love may be twisted and turned
in all sorts of ways; it may show itself in sadism or a desire
for humiliation or in even more remote forms, but always
behind it all is the need of the human being for love. Without
this basic datum human sexuality is simply not intelligible; we
cannot treat it as we can to a great extent treat other appetites,
in isolation from a man's relation to others.

I want to claim, then, that sexual desire in man is a matter
of sexual *love* and if we are to criticize some forms that the
satisfaction of this desire takes, it is by criticizing their relevance to love. Love is not added to sex; sex without love, or
sex with bogus or imitation love, is distorted in itself, one of
its essential elements is missing.

Let us then draw another picture and see if we can make it
an improvement on the one we have rejected. The root of the
sexual desire is, as in the other picture, the biological need for

the maintenance of the race, but this expresses itself in the individual not as an undifferentiated desire for sexual satisfaction but in a desire for union with another. "It is not good for man to be alone." As a matter of physiology and psychology this desire may suffer various vicissitudes in an individual; for one reason or another it may turn back upon the individual or it may turn to others of his or her own sex. We call these sexual desires abnormal not because they are uncommon but because they are not aligned with the general purpose for which in nature the sexual instinct exists. According, then, to the picture which I am drawing, sex, love and marriage are not three separate things which we are lucky if we find combined. They form one thing and if either sex or marriage exists in a state of separation from love or from each other they are imperfect parts lacking their own fulfilment.

What, then, do we mean by love? Love simply means desiring good for another person, it means shifting the centre of gravity of your desires so that it coincides with that of another person; this is why love involves union. Your desires are now focused on the happiness of another person. Just as at any time you might be prepared to forgo a lesser happiness for yourself for the sake of a greater one, so in love you are prepared to forgo any lesser happiness for the sake of your greatest happiness, which now coincides with the happiness, or what you think to be the happiness, of another. There are two things to notice here; first of all, love means a giving of yourself to another, but secondly, it does not mean a surrender of your personality to another. It does not mean that you eliminate the centre of your personality, it means that you strive that it should coincide with that of another. Thus you *could* surrender your personality to another by placing yourself completely in his hands—say by some kind of drugs or hypnosis—then what you did would be entirely governed by him, it would really be his activity. But in love, your actions, though done from the point of view of another, remain absolutely your own actions.

Love is self-sacrifice, not suicide. Love is essentially a thing of freedom, a matter of my spontaneous action. It is a transcending of the self; to be able to transfer the centre of yourself to coincide with that of another involves a kind of picking yourself up by your own bootlaces; you are not simply being carried away, you are carrying yourself away.

It is because a carrying-away-out-of-yourself is involved that love, in the sense in which we have been talking about it, has affinities with the intoxication of the feelings that accompanies it in sexual love. In sexual passion we have the sense of being carried away by something which is ours, our sexual powers, and which is yet stronger than we are. Sexual appetites belong to the individual but not for the sake of the individual; his eating and drinking are for his own existence, his sexual powers relate him to the whole race. They belong to our solidarity in time with the race. And so in sexual passion we have the feeling of being carried away by something in us which belongs to the whole race, which is greater than ourselves. The morphology of this feeling in a sense corresponds to that of love as we have been describing it. As we have seen it, love is a matter of spontaneity, of freedom of the will; it is an act by which we carry ourselves outside our own circle of needs and preferences; and this pattern is repeated in the emotions by the passion of love. Thus we can say similar things about them— for example, that sexual passion is in a sense unselfish, it is not grasping and mean as are some of our desires. Nevertheless sexual passion is only an image of love, drawn in the emotions, just as intoxication can be a picture of freedom and happiness.

When we discuss marriage we have first to discuss its "normal" form, that is, its complete form, then we can come to consider various defects to which it may be subject. Marriage as a norm is the sexual union of two people who love each other; that is to say, their giving of themselves to each other includes the sexual union by which they give their bodies to each other, so that each can say of the other, "This is my body."

Sexual union exists, of course, to keep the race in being, and in this sense the purpose of marriage is the procreation of children. This is a purpose that marriage has quite independently of what a particular individual might want of it. The purpose of sleep is to rest and refresh us, it has this purpose as a matter of biology even though we may have all sorts of reasons for wanting to go to sleep—to avoid a boring talk, to forget about our worries, or whatever. We do not decide for ourselves what marriage, is for, any more than we decide for ourselves what *we* are for. Marriage *is* an institution which is already there in nature when we decide to go in for it. Just, as there are certain things we must not do to human beings because they are human beings whatever else they may be-employees, enemy soldiers, criminals etc.—so there are certain things we may not do to the institution of marriage just because it is the institution, whatever else it may be.

In the Book of Genesis, the first creation story makes man and women "to be fruitful and multiply and fill the earth", but the second story introduces woman because "it is not good for man to be alone." We can say that the purpose of marriage is the procreation of children, but we can also say that its purpose is the fulfilment of man and woman in love. There has been a certain amount of discussion in the past about the relative importance of these "two ends" of marriage. Some theologians have stressed the first and others have stressed the second. Some have said that the first is primary and the second secondary, others have retorted, "No, not secondary, *subsidiary*." What gives the whole discussion its slight air of unreality is that we know very well that the participants are really thinking about something else. One side is simply saying, "You must not make the personal fulfilment of husband and wife serve as an excuse for abusing the procreative function of marriage"; the other side is saying, "You must not make the procreation of children an excuse for selfishness, lovelessness and neglect in marriage." Both sides are obviously right and so the argument continues.

Marriage is not just the fact of two people living together in sexual love, it is man and wife living together in love which involves sexual love, it is a total giving of each to the other and as such it demands a commitment. In marriage a man gives to his wife everything that is his, including his body, his whole life; that is why marriage takes the form of a promise. In marriage a man dedicates the whole of his life to another. In marriage a man and woman make the extraordinary claim that they can establish a relationship of love which will be independent of what happens to them, which will transcend all the accidents that may occur. They establish a society of love which exists unconditionally. Human sexuality is properly speaking a function of this community of love; if it is exercised outside this communion it fails to be true human sexuality. Why is this so? Why could not true human sexuality exist in the context of, say, a temporary liaison? The reason is, to my mind, that sexuality is fundamentally the gift of one of the greatest things I have that I can give. I have greater things than my body but I cannot give them to another; the gifts of grace, the powers of my mind etc. I can use these for others but I cannot put them under their control. They belong to the spiritual centre of my personality which, as we saw, can be so transferred as to coincide with that of another, but cannot be taken over by another. There is one other thing I have that is greater than my body and which can be given up, and that is my life. And it is with life as it is with my body, I can give up my life in certain circumstances (in a context, of course, of love) and it is self-sacrifice, but if I give it up in lesser contexts it is suicide. To give my body for, say, three years and at the end demand a return is to degrade human sexuality by putting it on the level of lesser goods. It is selling something sacred, it is a kind of simony. If I am to give my body to another this can only be a gift in unconditional love and self-sacrifice, not a part of a transaction. It is for this reason that marriage is of its nature a permanent thing, because it is an unconditional thing.

If it is to be a personal commitment it must be accomplished by some sign of commitment. If the caveman drags the cave-girl into his cave, this may be marriage if it is in fact a conventional sign with a meaning, if it involves a commitment on his and her part. But if he is simply dragging her into the cave there is clearly no marriage. Any society will have established conventional signs for committing oneself to another. There will be some symbolic gesture which counts as having promised oneself unconditionally to another. Any such sign is a contract of marriage.

So far I have been dealing with sex and marriage; I have not said a word about the sacrament of marriage. This takes us into an entirely new dimension. When the Church says that marriage is a sacrament, she does not mean that she thinks marriage is a good thing, nor does she simply bless the marriage contract, nor is it simply that she regards a good married life as an occasion for God's grace. Not at all; when she says that Christian marriage is a sacrament she means it is a new kind of reality. The Christian family is a mystery, something we can only know about by faith. We do not see the Christian family with our bodily eyes, any more than men saw the divinity of Christ or they can see the outpouring of the Spirit in baptism. What they can see is the outward sign, the sacrament which represents the mystery that it contains. So far we have been considering marriage as belonging to the process of the human race; it belongs to our solidarity in time with our fellow men, it belongs to the evolution and history of mankind; but the marriage of Christians is something else: it is a part of the process of mankind towards God, and this process towards fulfilment in Christ, towards the Pleroma, is called the Church. Marriage is the only sacrament in which these two orders coincide in this way. The outward signs of the other sacraments are ritual gestures, things which have no natural value though they have, of course, a social value. We do not take a baby to the font to wash it, we do not go to Holy Communion because we are hungry, but marriage is the intersection of the biological and supernatural orders.

Marriage, then, is one of the seven signs, the symbolic rites which go to constitute the Church. In order to understand this more clearly we must know something about the meaning of a sacrament. A sacrament—as we have already seen—is a revelation of the divine plan of salvation which itself contains and furthers that salvation. The great sacrament is the humanity of Christ, the image of the unseen God, but we say too that the great events of the Old Testament were sacramental in that they were saving acts of God which showed forth the mystery of his plan. They spoke figuratively of the destiny of Israel which is Christ at the same time as they prepared the way for his coming. They symbolized what they effected. The sacraments of the New Law effect what they symbolize. Together they bring into being the Church, a new kind of reality, neither a physical thing that we can see with our eyes nor a concept that we can understand with our minds, but a mystery that we can know by faith. The sacraments affect us neither as physical causes, nor, on the other hand, as mere symbols appealing to our understanding; they affect us at the level of the mystery.

This may become clearer if we recall again the traditional theology of the sacraments. A sacrament involves three levels of reality:

(1) The *rite,* which can be *seen,* which symbolizes and when genuinely performed brings about
(2) The *sacramental reality* (the mystery), which is *known by faith* and which symbolizes and in a man of good dispositions brings about
(3) The *final reality,* union with God in love.

Thus:

BAPTISM

Rite	Sacramental Reality	Final Reality
Plunging in water, etc.	Incorporation in the Church, the kingdom of priests—Character.	Rebirth to divine life through the Spirit of love.

EUCHARIST

Sacred meal, etc.	Body of Christ given us for our food.	Unity of Mystical Body in love.

MARRIAGE

Dedication of bodily life to another etc.	Sacramental bond of marriage.	Personal appropriation of love uniting Christ and Church.

Let us look at these levels in turn. First of all, the contract of marriage is itself the sacrament, it is itself the outward sign. The marriage consists in the commitment by the man and woman concerned; any ceremonies or blessing that may surround it are quite accidental to the sacrament, like the ceremonies surrounding baptism or the eucharistic meal. It is the husband and wife who administer the sacrament to each other, each of them exercising the priesthood received in baptism. In comparatively recent years the Catholic Church has demanded of her own members that the contract of marriage should (apart from exceptional circumstances) be made in the presence of the parish priest and two witnesses. I said that any society will have established conventional procedures as a criterion of what is to count as a valid agreement, and this, then, is a requirement in this particular society. Needless to say, the legislation does not apply to those not in the society. Hence non-Catholic Christians can make a valid contract of marriage and thus enter into the sacrament of marriage, in any way recognized by society as valid—for example in a registry office. This is why the Catholic Church recognizes as valid the marriages of non-Catholics in a registry office, but not the marriages of her own children. This has nothing to do with the morals of the matter, it is a matter of the convention for what counts as a valid contract in a particular society. It is no good going around in white lace and orange blossom if the particular and proper convention of your society is to be dragged by the hair into a cave.

This contract is a symbol. How and what does it symbolize? Every sacramental sign, according to St. Thomas Aquinas, takes in, in its symbolism, the whole sweep of the divine plan. Looking to the past, it refers back to Christ's passion and through this to the great symbolic deeds of the Old Testament; looking to the present, it symbolizes a work of God, the realization of a sacramental reality, and through that the realization of divine love in a man; and looking to the future, it refers to the consummation of all things in the Second Coming. It is not difficult to see how this applies to marriage. In the marriage contract we have a symbol which is a favourite scriptural image of the dealings of Yahweh with Israel and of the coming of the Saviour. In every marriage we see represented the love of Yahweh for the Virgin Israel which is to make her fruitful; we see the marriage of the Holy Spirit and the Virgin Mary which bore fruit in Christ. Again, each marriage looks forward to the final consummation of the marriage between Christ and his bride the Church, when the Holy City comes down out of heaven adorned as a bride for her husband, as we read in the Book of Revelation.

And in the present the contract entered into between the man and woman symbolizes and brings into being a bond between them at the level of sacramental reality. This bond is stronger even than human love, stronger than the human contract which symbolizes it. It is such stuff as the Church is made on, it has the permanence and stability of the Church itself. Each marriage is a participation in the enduring bond which unites Christ to his bride. The forging of the bond of marriage is the work of Christ's love. In marriage we have what God has joined together—not merely by instituting marriage as a natural society, but by the power of a sacrament. Just as in baptism it is a man

who performs the outward rite but Christ himself who sancti-
fies the child, so in this sacrament it is a man and woman who
make the contract but Christ who joins them in a dimension
into which we cannot as yet reach, which we can know of only
by faith.

The marriage bond is as durable as the Church itself, indeed
it is a sharing in the stability of the Church, but it is not *more*
durable than the Church. The Church belongs to the sacramental era, to the interim period in which we await Christ's coming.
At that moment sacramental reality as something other than
natural reality will cease as the shadow disappears in the sun.
Of the new Jerusalem we read, "I saw no temple therein, for
the Lord God almighty is the temple thereof, and the Lamb."
It is for this reason that "there is no marrying nor giving in
marriage in heaven". At the end of time there will be a wither-
ing away of the Church; faith and hope and the sacraments
will disappear but charity will remain. And this is what we are
concerned with at the third level of the sacrament. It is thus not
strictly true to say, as D. H. Lawrence does, that the Catholic
Church teaches that marriage is eternal; but rather, that the
final fruits of marriage will be eternal. The attainment of the
grace of divine love which is the ultimate reality in the sacraments depends, as I have said, on the dispositions of the people concerned. If two people have so taken personal possession
of their marriage that they are united not just by contract, not
just by the sacramental bond, but by a mutual personal love
which is a unique and unrepeatable sharing in the divine love,
this bond between them lasts for eternity. This applies too, it
seems to me, to the whole family relationship, for marriage
is not just a matter of two people but of a community. If the
bonds which bind this community together are made personal,
then the family forms a community of divine love which transcends time and will last for eternity in heaven.

It must be remembered that what we are speaking of is love
in the sense of a self-transcendence, an attitude of the will by

which you carry yourself out of yourself to union with another person. We are not directly speaking of the emotional state which mirrors that love, but which also may be present without it. Being in love in this emotional sense is a normal emotional accompaniment of genuine other-directed sexual desire, and for this reason it is usually possible for most people to fall in love with almost anybody who is not actively repulsive. Children have this love for their parents and vice versa; another variation of it occurs in adolescent homosexuality; and yet another when the boy meets the girl. At every stage of being in love, the problem is always to convert the emotional into the reality which it mirrors. Being in love with someone is a good way to begin loving them, it gives you a useful start, but it demands development or it will remain infantile and self-centred. These are platitudes for anyone concerned with education. Education has to be first of all a matter of opening a person to the possibility of love. It is not so clearly recognized that this is also true of marriage. The enormous propaganda pressure to which we are subjected, designed to make us think of marriage as the end of a story (a propaganda kept up by people who make money out of others being infantile), can blind us to the human fact that marriage is usually the beginning of a more important story. It is the beginning of an era in which two people slowly and painfully learn to love each other, in which they discover in experience that sexuality in marriage is by no means a repetition of sexual experiments outside marriage, that sex divorced from married love is just a bogus imitation marriage, a defective sexuality. Now in Christian marriage this process of growing in human love continuously reflects and realizes a growth in divine love. In Christian marriage man and woman become in a yet deeper sense images of God. In their natural human lives they image God in that they are more like God than other creatures are, but now they imitate God by possessing and exercising a divine life.

The divine life comes to Christ's fellow men through his resurrection, and such is the human condition that the Resurrection demands the Cross. Love is a total giving, it is a sacrifice, and in a world still twisted by the Fall sacrifice involves some form of immolation. If we find the glory of the risen Christ in Christian marriage we also find the Cross. In theory there is no reason why a marriage should not be a matter of human happiness and satisfaction reflecting and realizing a growing bond of divine love; but in actual fact the divine love grows usually only at the expense of much human happiness. There are few marriages of which it could be said that there has not been a time when human love has been reduced to its stark fundamentals, a cold and comfortless choice between loyalty and betrayal. Here in the darkness of faith are the moments of real growth in the divine love which is to bind husband and wife together for eternity. But it does not feel like that. In these moments of crisis we can only triumph by the power of Christ's cross.

Finally, a word about non-sacramental marriages. I have said that a contract of marriage between baptized Christians is the sacrament of marriage. What of those who are not baptized? Is there the possibility of an enduring bond of divine love between, say, pagans who marry?

Here, I think, we can apply the same principles that we do to baptism when we speak of baptism of desire. If a man who wishes to be baptized is for some reason prevented from doing so, the second-level reality is not realized in him, he does not become a member of the cultic community, the Church. He cannot, for example, actually offer the eucharistic sacrifice in the way that the baptized can. He does not share in the priesthood of the Church. Nevertheless it is the constant tradition of the Church that, in virtue of his desire for baptism, the third and ultimate level of reality, the grace of Communion in the Holy Spirit, is realized in him. This is called baptism of desire;

not a special sort of baptism, but a desire for an ordinary sort of baptism. It is also traditionally recognized that desire for baptism may take very mysterious forms; it does not have to be an explicit formulated desire. It is increasingly recognized that, for all we know, something which amounts to a desire for baptism may be present in someone who has never heard of baptism. It is an important point, however, that we do not in such cases *know*. The pagans may not be in the outer darkness but we are in the dark about whether they are or not. To be invisibly united to the Church is to be *invisibly* united to her. Now it seems to me that we can say the same of a pagan marriage. In such a case, again, the second-level reality would be missing, the sacramental bond. This is the reason why it is possible in certain extraordinary circumstances for such a marriage to be dissolved.

But once more bypassing the second level, it seems to me that by an implicit desire for the sacrament a pagan husband and wife might receive the reality at the fundamental level, the reality of participation in the divine love which unites Christ to his bride, the Church. It must be emphasized, however, that the final reality at the third level is something we cannot detect with any certainty. The Christian cannot even be certain that he himself is in a state of grace, still less can he know about the secret workings of divine love in the soul of a man who shows none of the sacramental signs of that love.

9

LIFE AFTER DEATH

IN this book I have been considering different aspects of the Church—in particular, seeing how it is constituted by the sacraments. In this chapter I shall look at the theology of death, judgement, and the life to come, in order to set out the end for which the Church exists.

Christians and humanists are in agreement about so much—at any rate, one kind of Christian and one kind of humanist are in agreement about so much—that it is worth while pointing to an issue which absolutely divides them. It seems to me that the opposition between the two views of man is most sharply brought out in their attitudes towards death. You may feel this is an unfair choice of battlefield, because in fact humanists hardly have an attitude to death. They haven't thought much about it, whereas Christians have thought rather a lot about it. But this very fact is the first point of difference between us: Christians think that nothing in life matters more than death, whereas humanists don't attach any special significance to it. To the humanist a preoccupation with death is either morbid or romantic. Death is an inevitable natural process; one should neither make a sombre fuss about it, as they do in Italy, nor a desperate attempt to pretend it hasn't happened, as they do in California. Death is or should be essentially a matter of public hygiene; we must be kind to the bereaved relatives and get rid of the body before it begins to smell. That is really all there is to it. Of course, a humanist does not have to advocate the clinical dreariness of the crematorium; he may very well feel that the traditional ceremonies of death are of value to society, that they provide an accepted framework within which personal grief can be contained. In this way the *Dies Irae* or *South*

Rampart Street Parade are justified by their relation to life, not death. Death is an incident in a man's life which happens to have a great effect on the lives of others; it need have no more significance for the man himself than any other incident in his life. Death is merely one moment among many, it just happens to be the last of the series. As we may treasure the last letter written by a dead friend, so we may pay special attention to his last moments of life, but they have no intrinsic special interest. A man's greatest work may have been over many years before his death. The high point in his life when he was most vital, most *there,* may be long in the past. Death may be simply a tidying up of the remains. I read recently a biography of Florence Nightingale and discovered to my astonishment that she did not die until 1910. Her extraordinary impact on the world was long past, according to her biographer.

> In 1901 darkness closed in on her. Her sight failed com-
> pletely . . . at the same time her mind began to fail . . . she
> lay for hours in a state of Coma . . . After February 1910
> she no longer spoke. The iron frame which had endured the
> cold and fevers of the Crimea, which had been taxed and
> driven in forty years of gigantic labours, still lived on,
> deprived of memory, of sensation, of sight, but still alive.
> The end came on August 13.

Now, the humanist will very naturally regard the actual physical death as a relatively trivial occurrence in the life of Miss Nightingale, and this, I think, is his real clash with the Christian. For the Christian the most significant thing in Miss Nightingale's life was what happened on 13 August 1910, far more important than all her labours for the British Army, for hospitals, and for India. The Christian will of course admit that the socially significant part of Miss Nightingale's life was finished well before her death, but for him the significance of her life cannot in the end be assessed by reference to her position in this society, only by reference to her position in the community of charity.

A philosophical moralist asked to judge between, say, Dr. Schweitzer and Hitler, would weigh up the good deeds of one against the wicked deeds of the other—always supposing he was prepared to pass any judgement at all. He might say that Dr. Schweitzer is a good man because in spite of one or two failings here and there and the odd human weakness, his life has on the whole been a record of good works, sincere love for his fellow men and intellectual integrity. His judgement would be arrived at by weighing the good deeds against the bad. This same idea of judging a life by weighing good deeds against sins is sometimes, rather surprisingly, to be found in medieval representations of the judgement of a soul—you see a pair of scales with the devil heaping sins into one side, with good deeds, or sometimes the soul itself, sitting in the other pan. I say this is surprising because it completely misrepresents the Christian idea of judgement—this is not at all a matter of weighing good against bad. It is fair enough to pass judgement, if you must, on the life of a man by assessing his different activities, but for the Christian the Judgement is not a judgement on a man's life but a judgement on the man himself. This judgement is death.

For the Christian a man's eternal fate depends not on the balance of good and evil in his life but on whether or not he has in him the power of divine love at his death. This seems a shocking doctrine when we first realize what it says. So I want now to try to explain how it makes sense. The whole of life is a preparation for death because it is only from death that eternal life can spring. Death is critical, I suggest, because a man is called upon to make death his act, to make it a sacrificial offering, and this he can only do by the divine power of charity in him. Without this death will not be his own; he will never accept death, and this is damnation. In other words, I take *literally* the idea that a man must lose his life in order to save it. What is required of every man is that he should die through love for the Father, as Christ did on the Cross. This notion may become clearer later on.

Because of the fall of man the transition from secular to sacred is through death, there is no other way; death, which is the punishment of fallen man, has become, because of the Cross, the way to resurrection and new life. To understand this we must first try to get clear the relation between the old world of corruption and the new world of divine life, the relationship between the corruptible flesh in which Christ became incarnate and which he shared with us and the glorious body in which he rose from the dead, which we are to share with him.

In the first place we must notice that we have here a genuine passing over, not a substitution. It is the same body that died on the Cross and is now in glory, a real human body, part of our race. This is surely part of the point of the strange story about Thomas putting his fingers in the prints of the nails. But in the second place, this same body is now transfigured into new life. It is important to hang on to both these facts. What it means is that our flesh, our natural life, is not just the *opposite* of the risen life, for it is this human flesh that is going to be transfigured, it is not going to be wiped out and replaced by something else. This is why traditional Catholic theology resists the identification of nature with sin. It is true that our natural life is sinful—this is what we mean by the doctrine of the Fall—but it is not, as some Christians have said, the same thing to be natural and to be sinful. It was not just from a corrupt affection for pagan philosophers that the Catholic Church stood out against the Reformers' teaching that nature is utterly corrupt. She was not resisting the Protestant idea in the name of Aristotle and natural law, but in the name of her theology of the Redemption. The transition to the risen world demands that we deny both sin and nature, that we repent and that we die. It is important to see that these are not the same sort of denial. Sin is the sheer opposite of grace; it is simply abjured and there is an end to it, it has no root of good in it. In the baptismal ceremony we simply renounce Satan and turn to Christ; there is no sense in which sin is redeemed. But the flesh is not abjured. It is denied only that it may rise again. It is this mortal flesh that puts on incorruption.

Thus because of the Fall the flesh is at odds with divine life, and it is for this reason that it is through *death* that we are saved. We can see the redemptive act of Christ as a passing-over from the life of perishable flesh to new life, but because of the distortion in the fabric of creation this movement is dialectical; it is not a smooth transition from old to new, and the flesh must be crucified in order to rise again. In St. John, Christ refers to his passion as his consecration; he is set aside and made sacred, he is sacrificed. In a fallen world sacrifice implies dying to the profane in order to belong to the sacred.

What is required of the Christian is that he make the same journey as Christ. If he is to live the new life in Christ he must die as Christ did. For the Christian, death is the supreme moment of any man's life just because it was the supreme moment of Christ's life. It was his "hour", as he calls it in St. John, it was the whole purpose of his coming. Everything in his life leads towards his "lifting up"; throughout St. John we are reminded of the approach of this hour which is to give meaning to all he does. If we are to be one with Christ in his mission we must be one with him in death, his death and ours.

There are several senses in which we can be said to unite ourselves with Christ's death. We do so sacramentally in baptism—for as many as are baptized in Christ Jesus are baptized in his death. That is to say, we symbolize our death to the world and in doing so share sacramentally, but only sacramentally, in the risen life. Secondly, we can die metaphorically in Christ; that is to say, we can deny ourselves, practise mortification (make ourselves dead)—this is what we do in Lent (part of the time anyway). Thirdly, and most importantly, we can literally and physically die in Christ—it is this that is above all demanded of us.

I should like at this point to say a little more about what I have called "metaphorical" death in Christ. We do not really die during Lent, but we so to speak rehearse for death, we prepare ourselves to accept death. Giving up various things that we want and cling to is a sort of flexing the muscles to give up the thing we cling to most of all, our lives. Martyrdom comes less easily to the self-indulgent man, and not only the self-indulgent man but the man who has not denied himself. But even though we have the authority of St. Paul for comparing self-denial with athletic training, it is not this psychological effect on us that matters first of all. The primary value of mortification lies in the fact that it is a way of uniting ourselves with the suffering Christ. It is because this voluntary anticipation of death is an expression of love that it has its first value. The fact that it leaves us a little more detached from ourselves, is a secondary thing—though of some significance, as we shall see later, for the doctrine of purgatory. Let me repeat this to get it clear: Penance is first of all valuable as an expression of charity and one by which our love is fostered and grows, but it also has the effect of making us a little less bound up in self. Now it will I hope be clear that the second of these effects is not possible without the first. Penance which is not performed through love of God and man not only does not increase our charity but it does not detach us from ourselves. On the contrary, we become even more tied up in ourselves in yet subtler ways. This business of being tied up in oneself is going to be important later. At this point it is probably worth pausing to notice the difference between the Christian idea of self-denial and the philosopher's idea of self-control.

A man who is concerned with the good life will recognize the importance of self-control. It is necessary to strike a civilized mean between overindulgence in what we like and a harsh and barbarous repression of our desires. The educated man will be moderate in his pleasures and not enslaved by them. This is an admirable ideal that would be accepted by humanists and Christians alike, but it is not what a Christian means by self-denial. It is not, of course, that the Christian disapproves of self-control; it is just that he means something different by mortification. He will also point out that self-control which is not animated by charity will soon stiffen and die, but that is another point. The essential difference is that whereas the philosopher as such is concerned with the good life, the Christian is concerned with death. Whereas self-control has its value because by it a man lives well, self-denial has its value because by it a man dies well.

The point of contact between the philosophical moralist and the Christian is not to be found here. The analogy of the Christian life is not to be found in the philosopher's account of the good life, but in the philosopher's account of what would seem to be a very unusual kind of life, the life of the hero, of the man who gives up life rather than betray his standards. Most people would recognize that there can be circumstances in which the good life involves the choice of death. This is the kind of thing that happens to resistance workers and revolutionaries and other outstandingly heroic men. It is not, to all appearances and so far as the philosopher can see, the common lot of man. Most of us will die in our beds or in street accidents or blasted by the Bomb, some few of us will no doubt be hanged, but in any case it will be an unavoidable business; it is a minority who choose death for their convictions.

Now I am saying that according to the Christian message all men are really required to lay down their lives in this way. The real world, as it is revealed in the light of faith, is an heroic world. There is no casual death, there is only a choice between martyrdom and betrayal. If this were true then it would be clear death holds its special significance for the Christian. If the only way to be saved is through physical martyrdom then obviously the actual moment of death is, as the Spaniards say, the moment of truth, deciding a man's eternal fate.

We should now pause for a moment and consider the utter implausibility of what I am suggesting. In the first place, not only are very few people actually martyred for the Faith, but an actual majority of canonized saints are not martyrs. And whatever we may feel about the right of the Church to declare a man to be a saint, it seems (to say the least) odd to have a Christian theory of sanctity which excludes from heaven not only St. Augustine, St. Thomas Aquinas and St. Francis but also the Virgin Mary—the fact that it allows in King Charles I is at best a minor consolation. It would seem therefore false to hold that to be saved we must die as martyrs.

In answer to this objection I should say that what essentially makes a man a martyr is not the publicity surrounding his death but the attitude he takes towards it. A martyr is a man who gives up his life for the love of God. The paradigm case of this is the man who is offered a free choice between dying and doing something contrary to the love of God—in such circumstances the nature of the business is clear. It is this sort of case that defines the attitude of mind in question. I mean this: If you had to describe what it is to be someone's friend, you would probably describe the sort of things you would expect a friend to do—the kind of behaviour that would lead us to say, Fred is a friend of Charlie, whereas George is not. Now it is of course possible in particular circumstances for Fred to be a friend of Charlie and yet not to show any of this behaviour. Nevertheless what we mean by friendship is described by describing the normal or paradigm case. Now martyrdom is, I am suggesting, the paradigm case of sanctity, and it may be for this reason that the first saints to be honoured in the Church were the martyrs. Martyrs in fact are not a special kind of saint, but every saint is some kind of martyr. What is common to all saints is a certain way of taking death. A martyr does it publicly, another saint may do it privately. But in both cases there is an actual abandonment of life, a positive willingness to die, and this is required for sanctity. There is, of course, an obvious objection to this view: one afternoon some months ago I found myself being driven at about 50 m.p.h. along the centre lane of the Watford by-pass, and I was interested to see a lorry also occupying the centre lane coming in the opposite direction—in the two or three seconds before impact I did not decide whether or not I was willing to accept death; instead I was working out the best position for my legs (about which I have come to think I may have miscalculated). Now, under only slightly different conditions I should now be exceedingly expert about the next world, though unable to pass on the information. Yet it seems on my theory that since I had no chance voluntarily to accept death as a martyr does, I could not have been saved.

There is much to be said about this objection, but before dealing with it I should like to look at another point which might be raised. I have said that sanctity demands a positive willingness to die, and it may be asked, Does this mean that all suicides are saints? This is not merely a frivolous point, for in the difference between suicide and martyrdom lies a difference between two whole approaches to life and death. The Christian is often accused by people like Robert Graves of rejecting life, of finding no value in transitory and created things, of undervaluing human love and ordinary natural pleasures, of looking with suspicion on beauty and artistry. The true Christian is harsh and monkish, given to smashing statuary and refusing a drink. If in practice the Roman Church does not do this kind of thing it is only because she has been infected with creeping paganism. There are of course cultured clerics who go for Ingmar Bergmann and Brecht and Millicent Martin, but they don't really like any of this stuff; it is just bait to get you into the confessional.

Now, I think the people who believe this about Christianity, including, of course, some Christians, do so because in a sense they confuse martyrdom with suicide. The suicide chooses death because for one reason or another—and normally, I suppose, through some mental breakdown—he feels life to be insupportable. Life has become an enemy to be cheated by death. For the suicide life is hostile, and it is this sort of hostility to life that is expressed in what is commonly called puritanism. For the suicide death is a means of escaping from life, for the martyr it is a means of offering his life. The suicide and the martyr have it in common that neither of them thinks of life as an absolute good. In this they both reject a facile humanism, and it is perhaps for this reason that the optimistic humanist, seeing them both as enemies, confuses them together. Christian humanism, then, implies a delight in the good things of this world combined with a willingness to sacrifice them all for the absolute good. It is just because of their value that the sacrifice is meaningful. It is not just a case of being prepared if necessary to give up what we value—if it comes to the point of choosing. For everyone it does come to the point, everyone actually has to give up absolutely everything, for this is what happens when you die. We have all had experience of minor or major deprivations. Some of us have tried to give up smoking for Lent; those of us who have been in prison will have had similar deprivations; now, death is the taking away not just of this or that luxury or necessity, but of everything. It is the loss of the body, the loss of all communion with our fellow men, the loss of all new experience or imagination. It is a kind of absolute solitary confinement in the dark. Annihilation, you might say, would not be so bad, for there would be nothing left to be deprived, but in fact we have hanging over us the horrible threat of immortality. Death means that we survive deprived of everything. I have spoken of self-denial as a detachment from self; death is the loss of self, total abandonment. What is required of man is that he makes this abandonment his own act, an act of sacrifice in union with the act of Christ on the Cross. If he fails to make death his own act, it remains his enemy. If it is his own act he passes through it in

Christ to resurrection, if he does not he suffers death as an enemy for eternity.

Let us now return to the objection I put a little while ago: that all this seems to demand a highly conscious and wideawake approach to death. If I were conscious in my last moments, ideally lying quietly in bed, not distracted by intense pain, and able to collect my thoughts, then, no doubt, I could accept my death and offer it sacrificially in union with Christ, but in fact most deaths are either quicker or messier than this and quite a lot of people simply die in their sleep. Do I have to postulate that everyone is miraculously given the necessary few moments of consciousness before death (even when they obviously aren't) or do I have to say that everyone who dies suddenly or unconscious is damned?

In order to answer this question we have to see that the act of dying is beyond our human powers. This absolute self-sacrifice requires a self-transcendence of which we are not capable. What is required of us is not just that we die, not even that we die voluntarily, but that our death be an expression of divine love. We must become "obedient unto death" in charity, and this, of course, like any other divine act, is only possible through the divine life that we share in grace. In other words, the act of death is possible to us only through grace; like faith, it is something that exceeds our capabilities.

The act of death that I do is, then, first of all an act of God in me; it is only secondarily my own act. It is first of all a result of the fact that I am in Christ. Now, to have the divine life in me normally means to do human acts which are also divine. To share the life of Christ involves expressing divine love in our actions. But what sort of human behaviour will follow from my possession of divine life depends on my human condition. The expression of divine life in a child of six is not the same as its expression in a man of thirty, a man filled with divine love does not behave the same way when he is asleep and when he is awake, when he is sane and when he goes mad—in other words, the mere fact that he is asleep or very young or insane does not mean that God cannot act in and through him. The obvious example here is that of infant baptism. Belief in the efficacy of infant baptism depends on the belief that what happens, in baptism is first of all an act of God, not an act of man. Adult baptism naturally demands of the adult a proclamation of the Faith which it brings him, for he is humanly able to proclaim it. Faith for him is something articulate, something he understands to some extent. In the infant the same faith is present in the way suited to an infant— unconscious, radically present, not yet formulated.

Now I would suggest that when a Christian dies "in a state of grace", filled with divine love, if he is conscious it is a bit like an adult baptism—the effect of grace will be for him personally and consciously to make the act of self-abandonment, the act of death. But if he is unconscious or frenzied with pain, grace will still take its effect though in a different human mode. The deciding factor is not the conscious effort we make but the work of God in us.

It will be clear then that in death, as in baptism, there are two things to be considered: the act of God and the act of man brought about by this act of God. When a child has been baptized, because of the act of God he possesses radically the Christian faith, but he needs religious teaching of some kind so that he may come to possess his faith in an adult and fully human way. Education does nothing to the faith but it does something to the child who has it.

Now, divine act and human acceptance are in the same way two elements in death. If a man dies unconscious there remains still his human acceptance of death, his human realization of the self-abandonment that death involves—this, I believe, is Purgatory. For the man who has consciously and absolutely performed his death, given up his life entirely to God, there is of course no Purgatory—hence the Christian tradition that Purgatory is not for martyrs. But the man who has not been able to do that in this life must do it in death. It is important to see that in Purgatory the decision has already been made; Purgatory is the vestiges of death, not a new opportunity to die. Purgatory is not an extension after death of the time available for decision, it is the realization of the consequences of the decision to die, to be totally self-denied. Purgatory is a sort of time of penance, of loss of self. The difference between purgatory and Lent is just this. The penances of Lent are a voluntary anticipation of death, performed for love of God, and as such they help to foster in us the life of love. Lent makes us love God more. Purgatory is not something we take upon ourselves in this way, but an inevitability that we have to face; it is not something we do freely and spontaneously, and hence it does not lead to any increase in our love—purgatory, as theologians say, is not meritorious.

Because purgatory means wrenching ourselves away from ourselves, because it means an absolute self-denial, its difficulty will depend on how closely we are bound up in ourselves—it will depend, in fact, on the sort of life we have led. If when we come to die we are fairly detached from ourselves then the self-abandonment of death will not come so hard—either as a conscious act at the hour of death or, if we die unconscious, as the realization of purgatory. The thing which will make us detached from ourselves is contrition, sorrow for our sins, mortification. The thing that binds us closer to ourselves and our lives is sin. Every time we sin we choose our own way rather than that of God and every sin makes us in this sense more selfish. Even though God in his mercy comes to us to give us the grace to repent, so that our sin no longer cuts us off from him, the psychological effects of the sin may remain—it is easier to commit that sin again than it was before. We have to do quite a lot of work to undo the damage we have done to ourselves by sin, even after the essential damage to our relationship with God has been repaired. If we neglect this work during life then facing the fact of death is much more difficult.

Thus, although the Christian must insist that the vital judgement, the decision between heaven and hell, depends not on how he lives but on how he dies, depends on whether he has in him at the moment of challenge the grace to die in Christ or not, nevertheless he also holds that in a secondary sense his fate in the next world does depend on how he has lived, for the difficulty of purgatory depends entirely on what sort of man he has made of himself—the more self-indulgent he is the more bitter is the self-abandonment required of him.

Now what of hell? I think it is important, in trying to present a picture of hell, to have some idea of how the picture is to be used, what aspect of the matter it is supposed to illuminate. There are basically two pictures of hell, both of which I think valuable, but valuable in different ways—it is disastrous when one picture is used to do the work of the other. The first picture is of hell as a lake of burning sulphur with devils, pitchforks and the rest of it—a most useful picture. The second is the picture of hell as what I shall call the "undead", the incapacity to accept death. I have read only one good book about damnation, *Pincher Martin* by William Golding. Those who know it will remember the inability to submit to "the black lightning"— this is the second picture.

When our ancestors talked of hell they were concerned about the character of man, but when we talk about it we are frequently concerned about the character of God. This is what makes the pictures. From the point of view of the character of man the important thing about the picture of hell is that it should be a thing to avoid, and this is admirably shown forth in the notion of boiling sulphur. Most normal people would be frightened of falling into a vat of boiling sulphur and would do almost anything to avoid this. The picture implies that this is a sensible attitude towards hell. If one is setting out to paint this sort of picture of hell, a picture to be used in this way, then it is merely silly to let the sulphur cool a little or give the damned souls a tea-break—the *point* of the picture is its nastiness.

The mistakes begin, however, when we use this old-fashioned type of picture as a clue to the character of God. If God is the kind of person who enjoys pushing people into boiling sulphur, he must be a maniac. This is not adult behaviour at all. And so we have another picture of hell, this time a picture which stresses what was left on one side in the other one—that hell is a state we get ourselves into without any help from God at all. God does not make hell, we do. Let me here repeat the warning about using the pictures in the wrong way. It is no good using the second kind of picture as a substitute for the first, to do the same kind of job. The second kind of picture is not dealing with the nastiness of hell. So if someone says, "Hell is absolute isolation", or something of the kind, then we are simply muddled if we say, "Oh, I'm so relieved, I'm sure I could stand that a lot better than burning sulphur." If, after examining the concept of hell, cutting out the mythological and metaphorical bits, one comes to the conclusion that it may not be so bad after all, then clearly one has gone wrong somewhere, for part of the point of hell is that it would be just as bad after all. If we say that we make our own hell then there is the temptation to think that we won't make it so bad for ourselves, and that is why the boiling sulphur picture is a valuable one to have as well.

The fire of hell is God. God is terrible and no man can look upon him and live, he is a consuming fire. To be safe in the presence of God you must be yourself sacred, you must share in God's power and life. To have to come into the presence of God without this protection is damnation. That is one picture of hell, the fundamental biblical one—the other biblical theme is based on the idea of hell as a rubbish dump smouldering away like Gehenna outside Jerusalem.

But hell is also the inability to accept death. The damned man is he who does not die in Christ, for whom death is therefore not a means of resurrection to new life. He is not able to make the act of self-sacrifice required of him. He is unable to

see why he should. I picture the damned as spending their time
continually justifying themselves to themselves, constantly
showing how right they were and why they have no need to
repent.

> In the small circle of pain within the skull
> You still shall tramp and tread one endless round
> Of thought, to justify your action to yourselves
> Weaving a fiction that unravels as you weave
> Being forever in the hell of make-believe.

All the souls in hell, I think, are quite convinced that they have
been damned unjustly. The analogy I find most useful is that
of the child who has lost his temper and is sulking. He wants,
of course, to return to the affection of his friends, but he is
blowed if he is going to apologize, his pride keeps him out
even though he wants very much to return. Everybody is fully
prepared to receive him back if only he will make the gesture
of returning, but this he finds himself unable to do. He cannot
perform the self-abandonment required. He is unable to die.

Anyone in hell who was sorry for his sin would of course
instantly be in heaven; the point of hell is that this does not
happen. If it did hell would be nothing more than the prolon-
gation of the life of the sinner, and death would be no judgement at all. Death would not reveal sin for what it is—the
paralysis of will which makes love impossible. We must
remember that every time we repent of serious sin in this life
we do so only in consequence of a special intervention of
divine grace. Sin, like suicide, we can do all by ourselves, but
once the life is gone we no longer have the power to help
ourselves; we can kill ourselves but we cannot come back
from the dead ourselves. The very first beginnings of our
desire to have a desire to be sorry for our sins is an intervention by God, the beginning of a resurrection from the dead.
Life is a countless series of these gratuitous interventions of
mercy, none of which we deserve, to none of which we have

any right at all. They happen through our union with the body of Christ, our living bodies are in touch with him; when we come to die, the way we are united with him is through dying in him. If we fail to do this the channel of grace is no more. We are left with ourselves and our self-righteousness, confronted by God but unable to die into him.

I have spoken of purgatory and of hell, and perhaps I should finally say something of heaven. But in fact I have already done what is possible in previous chapters when I discussed the sacraments. For in our sacraments our faith is not merely a mental reaching out to what is to come; rather, we make contact with what is really present now. In them we are united now to the risen body of Christ. This is what we mean when we say that our sacraments are not just ordinary symbols—as were, for instance, those under the Old Law—for what they signify is present. Of course heaven is not present to us in the sacraments as it will be after the resurrection. It is, as we say, present in sacrament, in mystery, available to us only in faith— present to us through being symbolized, but none the less present in reality and not merely in the sense that we are thinking of it.

If you ask a Christian for his account of heaven, his best answer is to point to the sacraments of the Church:

> Unless you eat the flesh of the Son of Man and drink his blood you have no life in you; he who eats my flesh and drinks my blood has eternal life, and I will raise him up on the last day.

The Eucharist has an intrinsic relationship to the next world, so much so that the next world is best defined as what the Eucharist realizes and shows forth.

We do not know what the next world will look like, for our sacramental prophecies, like most prophecies, do not tell us that kind of thing. Just as the Pasch or the songs of the Suffering Servant did not foretell what the passion and resurrection of Christ would look like, but rather proclaimed what it would mean, so the Eucharist does not show us what the communion of our bodies in the risen Christ will look like. But we do know it will be a matter not of souls or spirits or ghosts, but of real corporeal human beings, though the condition of the body may, as St. Paul says, be as different from our present perishable state as is the plant from the seed.

10

A ROYAL PRIESTHOOD

S OME eople think that what is called the First Epistle
of St. Peter is not a letter but an address given by the
leader of the first Christian bishops to a group of men
and women who had just been baptized. Certainly a good deal
of it is devoted by St. Peter to an explanation of what it means
to have become a Christian:

> You are a chosen race, a royal priesthood, a holy nation,
> God's own people, that you may declare the wonderful
> deeds of him who called you out of darkness into his marvel-
> lous light. Once you were no people but now you are God's
> people . . . [1 Peter 2.9–10.]

The converts who listened to this would have recognized that
St. Peter's words are based on a famous passage in the Book
of Exodus. He is comparing the new community to which they
belong to the community of Israel:

> Yahweh called to Moses out of the mountain saying, "Thus
> you shall say to the house of Jacob, and tell the people of
> Israel:
> You have seen what I did to the Egyptians
> how I bore you on eagles' wings and brought you to myself.
> Now therefore if you will obey my voice and keep my
> covenant,
> you shall be my own possession among all peoples;
> for all the earth is mine and you shall be to me a kingdom
> of priests and a holy nation. [Exod. 19.3–6.]

Israel has not come to Yahweh of its own accord and by its
own power, Yahweh has brought it to himself. He did this by

defeating their oppressors at the Exodus; he has given them a law to guide them and made a covenant with them. These three things, Exodus, Law and Covenant, are the foundation of the People of the Old Testament. The People have been created for a definite purpose; they are to be his priests, his sacred nation. Israel is to be his possession among all peoples, not because the other peoples do not belong to him ("for all the earth is mine") but because it belongs to him in a special way, as his priesthood. It is to represent God to all the peoples and to represent humanity before God. The priestly activity of Israel is not something distinct from her history, her wars and her political influence. It is as a people with an historical destiny that she stands as a mystery and a sign of God's concern for man. The Hebrews were not a people who happened to have certain "advanced" views about God; their religious beliefs were an interpretation of their own history.

As we have seen throughout this book, the things foreshadowed in the Old Testament are fulfilled first of all in the person of Christ. In his defeat of Satan and passage through death to life we have the real exodus of man from darkness to life; he himself is the Word which is fulfilment of the Law, and in his body the New Covenant is established which unites God and man.

Again, as we have seen, these things are represented sacramentally in the Church. The people to whom St. Peter is speaking have just, by baptism, participated in Christ's exodus; they have received his Spirit so that the New Law is written in their hearts, and in the Eucharist they celebrate the New Covenant in his body and blood. Because of this they too have become a royal priesthood and a sacred nation.

According to the Epistle to the Hebrews there is an essential difference between the Christian community and the community of the Old Law, or any other religious body. Under the Old Law there had to be a class of priests who kept up a daily series of sacrifices for the people; and the reason for this was that every sacrifice was inadequate. This priestly class, however, with its continual repetition of sacrifices, is no longer necessary, for we have one High Priest, Jesus Christ, who has once for all offered the perfect and adequate sacrifice. The Christian body will therefore be characterized by the absence of a special group of men called priests, separated off from the rest of the community. It is Christ who is the one Priest, though the community as a whole may share in his priesthood. It seems that in order to emphasize this the earliest Christians avoided using the word "priest" except when speaking of Christ himself or, as with St. Peter, of the Church as a whole. When they wished to refer to the officials of the community they called them "overseers", "elders" and "ministers".

Now it is notorious that the Roman Church is an exceedingly clerical affair. For many centuries she has spoken of her bishops and presbyters as "priests", and no other Christian body is more dominated by its priestly class. Can such a body claim to be the Christian community as envisaged in the Epistle to the Hebrews? To many of the Reformers the claim seemed obviously false; whatever differences of function there might have to be within the community, the absolute distinction between clergy and laity, as found in the Roman Church, seemed a denial of all that the New Testament stood for. To have mediators between God and man other than Christ himself is to deny that his mission has succeeded.

This book is not concerned with defence of the Catholic position but with explanation of it, and in this matter it is important to see what this position is not. In the first place, traditional Catholicism is in full agreement with the Reformers' doctrine that there is but one priesthood in the Christian Church, that of Christ himself. We go on to say that it is possible to speak, nevertheless, as St. Peter does, of the priesthood of the Church. This is not something alongside or additional to Christ's priesthood, it is our sharing in it. It belongs to the fullness of his priestly power that we should be able to participate in it. We touch here on a deep point of difference between the Catholic and the Reformed traditions. To the Reformers it always seemed that to attribute anything to man as his own was to derogate from what belongs to God. For the Church to claim to *have* divine life or the power of the priesthood as its own life and power is to deny that everything is absolutely and entirely from God. To the Catholic, on the other hand, it seems that to say that God can only make creatures who are passive before him is to lessen his divine dignity; it belongs to God and to God alone, who is closer to me than I am to myself, that his activity can be mine without ceasing to be his. This, however, is not the place to discuss this difference.

The clearest divergence between the Catholic teaching and that of the Reformers comes after this point, when we come to consider the organization of the Church itself. A man might agree that the Church is priestly and yet disagree with the next step that the Catholic takes. Such a man might hold that although the Church needs some kind of organization and some kind of authority within it, no particular form of organization is sacrosanct. What is appropriate at one stage in history need not be appropriate at another. For him the structure of the Church would be on the same level as, say, the architecture of her buildings or the language of her liturgy. In such matters it is well to respect a venerable tradition but nothing is fixed for all time.

The Catholic view is that the basic structure of the Church is one of her sacraments, part of her way of revealing Christ to the world and making him present in the world; it is on the level, that is to say, of baptism or the Eucharist. Just as a community which abandoned baptism in favour of some other initiation rite would not be the Christian Church, so one that lacked the structure and tradition of the episcopacy could not be that Church. We are speaking here, of course, of the basic structure. Just as the ceremonies and conventions surrounding baptism may change completely in the course of centuries and yet the sacrament itself be preserved, so everything associated with the priesthood may be altered and yet the thing itself remain. To insist on a fundamental qualitative distinction between the man who is ordained and the man who is not, is not necessarily to acquiesce in all the institutions and customs that have grown up around this distinction. The habit of subservience to the clergy, for example, that has developed in some countries, is no necessary part of the priesthood and is, indeed, highly dangerous to the Church.

In the traditional Catholic view the Church is not said to be a royal priesthood because it contains clergymen; on the contrary, it contains such ordained priests only because it is already priestly. My priesthood is derivative from, and a sacrament of, the priesthood of the whole body of Christians. At his ordination a man comes to represent sacramentally the community and Christ at the same time. The priesthood received at ordination depends upon the priesthood conferred by the character of baptism. What exactly is the difference between the priesthood of baptism and that of ordination? Before answering this question it may be useful to look at the matter of priesthood in a wider context.

Why Christianity should have a priesthood at all is part of the more general question, why it should be a religion at all. This is not easy to answer. By "religion" I mean the whole business of cult and worship; it has to do with the way in which man can get in touch with the divine. Religion is not, of course, magic (which is concerned with the control of dangerous and mysterious forces) and to criticize religious rites as though they were magical is crudely to misunderstand them but also to miss a more profound criticism that can be made of them. Religion is concerned with temples, sacrifices, feasts and prayers. Now, at first sight it might seem that Christ came to abolish religion. There can be no religion without some sort of distinction between the profane and the sacred, between the ordinary business of life and the special things, times, persons or places that have to do with the cult. A great deal of the teaching of Jesus seems devoted to breaking down this distinction. For him—and in this he stands well within the Hebrew prophetic tradition—a man is brought into the presence of his heavenly Father not, first of all, by religious observances, but by the quality of his ordinary relations with other people. It is not ritual that matters but love. He has come to destroy the Temple and the new temple that is to be rebuilt in three days is not made with hands, it is his risen body.

Nevertheless it is equally clear from the Gospels that Christ is not crudely humanist. Although he is obviously anti-clerical and even, in a sense, anti-religious, he does not appeal from religious rites to man's human nature. He does not teach that churches are unnecessary, all that is demanded of you is good behaviour. He demands of men that they receive the divine Spirit, and this is to be possible to them through belonging to a definite community, one that is at odds with the standards of behaviour expected by the world.

The paradox of the Gospels is due to the fact that Christ's mission is in one sense completed but in another sense awaits fulfilment at his second coming. In the meantime the Church is poised between the old world and the new. Certainly after our resurrection there will be no distinction of sacred and profane, no religious activity. We read in the Apocalypse that there will be no temple in the new Jerusalem, but the Church still awaits this consummation. On the other hand, the distinction of sacred and profane is no longer so simple as it was under the Old Law, when it more or less corresponded to the distinction between the Chosen People—the sacred nation—and the rest. Under the Old Testament grace was the history of the Hebrews; since the coming of Christ it can no longer be identified with history; grace is now the risen Christ who is not a part of history but its fulfilment.

The community of the Old Law and that after our resurrection both, so to say, exist for their own sakes. It is true that

Israel existed simply in order to prepare for and symbolize the Christ who was to come, but she did this simply by being herself, by maintaining her identity as a people and pursuing her historical destiny, by having a history alongside that of other peoples. Similarly, the risen world will exist for its own sake, it will simply be itself. But the Church in its present interim state represents the world to come but not simply by its history. The sacraments of the Church are historical but her history is not sacramental. There is in fact for her a distinction between her history, her "ordinary life", and her sacraments, a distinction corresponding to one between the profane and the sacred. Of course in the Old Law, too, there were "sacraments" in the sense of ceremonies such as the Passover or circumcision, or the sacrifices of the Temple, which were not part of ordinary life, but the significance of these was fundamentally social and historical, they were ultimately part of the political life of the Hebrews.

Thus in Christianity the distinction between the last things as realized and as yet to come takes the place of the distinction between profane and sacred that is to be found in other religions. None of the life of the Christian is profane, all his life except for sin is a realization of the eternal life within him, but not all of it is a sacramental revelation of that life. It is characteristic of Catholicism to make this distinction within the Christian life, a distinction quite other than that between sin and grace. Thus for the Catholic, the equivalent of the "profane" need not be the sinful.

But to return to the particular matter of the priesthood. All Christians, as we have seen, receive at baptism a character which is a membership in the worshipping community of the body of Christ and is thus a sharing in his priesthood. In virtue of this character they are, as St. Thomas Aquinas says, dedicated to the Christian cult. Again, in confirmation they receive a rededication, of which more in a moment; finally, by ordination a man shares in a special way in the priesthood of the Church.

How are we to define the precise difference that ordination makes?

Both the Christian who is ordained and the one who is not have become, by baptism, members of the laity, the *laos*, the People of God, and both have a priesthood. It is thus confusingly possible to speak of both as laymen and both as priests. For the sake of clarity, therefore, let us, in what follows, speak of the ordained man only as the priest and the other only as the layman. What, then, is the difference between the priesthood of the layman and that of the priest? In the convenient language of Thomism we might say that neither is said metaphorically to have a priesthood; it is literally true in both cases, but the word is used analogously, its primary application being to neither of them but to Christ. Such a schematic statement, however, conveys very little; let us instead consider the activity of both of them at Mass. The difference between the two is that the priest's offering of the Mass *qua* priest consists in certain sacramental acts, whereas the layman's offering need not do so.

The layman exercises his baptismal priesthood and offers the Mass to the extent that he is personally committed to what is taking place. The greater his devotion, the more truly he can be said to be offering the sacrifice. It is this personal element that defines his priestly activity. It is thus possible for him in special circumstances to offer the Mass without even receiving Communion. This sacramental act is not of itself essential to his offering. Similarly if, for example, he were deaf and dumb and paralysed he might genuinely offer the Mass without any external sign of participation in it. (It is, of course, strange that people in perfect health should sometimes behave at Mass as though they were afflicted in this way, but this is commonly due to ignorance or shyness and is not absolutely incompatible with a real offering of the Mass.) This offering of the Mass by exercise of the baptismal priesthood is the most important activity for anyone taking part, whether he be priest or layman;

without it the celebration of the Mass is quite worthless to them as individuals.

The layman is free to exercise his baptismal priesthood at Mass in a number of different ways, the priest can only exercise his priesthood by doing and saying certain definite things, for his offering consists in certain sacramental signs. It is of course necessary for the salvation of the priest, as for the layman, that the Mass should be an exercise of his baptismal priesthood—it would be a great wickedness to offer the Mass sacramentally without this. His sacramental priesthood should flow from his "personal" baptismal priesthood; the one without the other is rather like dead faith deprived of charity. Nevertheless the priest is not ordained precisely for his own salvation but for the community, and what he can do in virtue of his ordination is not first of all concerned with his own salvation but with the worship of the community. It is significant that we do not speak of the "sacrament of the priesthood" but of the "sacrament of order". Ordination establishes an order in the community, there is a special sense in which the community rather than the individual is the primary recipient of this sacrament. A man is not ordained for his own sake any more than he is married for his own sake. This does not mean that there are not definite specified persons who are married or ordained, nor does it mean that individuals may not receive definite graces from these sacraments, different from those received by other members of the community, but the sacrament exists in the first place for a community, in the one case the eucharistic assembly, in the other, the family.

Thus the priest's offering, precisely as a priest, is independent of his personal devotion and consists, unlike the layman's, in certain definite acts. If *he* were deaf, dumb and paralysed he would not be able to exercise his priesthood, for this depends on certain kinds of communication. We may put the same point another way by saying that both layman and priest represent Christ who offers the sacrifice, but the layman represents him in virtue of his personal devotion while the priest also represents him sacramentally. His actions symbolize sacramentally, and thereby make present, acts of Christ.

Besides speaking of representing Christ we can also speak of representing the Church. By their faith and personal commitment the congregation gathered at the Eucharist represent the Church. It is perfectly correct to say that they are the Catholic Church for a particular region. But the priest—or rather the bishop, who is priest in the fullest sense—represents the Church sacramentally; the Church is to be defined by reference to him. It is where the bishop is that the Church is. Even when we return to the ancient practice in which the bishop is elected by the laity, his consecration will make him no longer simply the representative of their choice but of their priesthood—he will represent them not precisely because they have chosen him but because he represents Christ, who has chosen them. Similarly, under the present system bishops are not merely the representatives of those who appoint them— I suppose it need hardly be said that bishops have never, in Catholic teaching, been thought of simply as agents of Rome, any more than the other Apostles were agents of St. Peter.

The priesthood, and in particular the episcopacy, cannot be described simply in terms of the sacramental action of the Eucharist. With the eucharistic sacrifice the Church has always associated the liturgy of the word—the first part of the Mass, in which the Scriptures are proclaimed and explained. Here there is an obvious difference of function between the bishop and his people. The tradition of the Church, the tradition of the Scriptures, exists in the whole community; it is not a secret doctrine handed down amongst a class of priests. The bishop, however, is the guardian of this tradition; he is, as we say in the Canon of the Mass, the "husbandman" of the apostolic and orthodox faith, the *cultor*. It is his business to see that it grows well and neither withers nor is choked with weeds. It belongs to him, then, first of all, to preach the Gospel to his people, and it is from this that he derives his teaching authority. This does not mean, of course, that the bishop is a substitute for biblical scholarship or for theologians, but it is his business and final responsibility to use the work of such men to foster the faith of his people and at the same time to ensure that no teaching conflicts with the faith of the whole community that has been handed down to him to preserve. A bishop may do his job badly, the faith of his people may remain infantile and stunted, his Church may fall into heresy or schism; we have no guarantee that this will not happen, it is only the faith of the Church as a whole, speaking through the assembly of all the bishops or through their leader the Bishop of Rome, that is guaranteed against failure.

It is not particularly difficult to understand the relationship and difference between the priesthood of the laity as a whole and that of the bishops and priests; a much more difficult question is the exact meaning of the priesthood derived from confirmation. Confirmation is a completion or ratification of baptism, and one of the reasons why it is a little obscure is that it is difficult to disentangle from that sacrament. In the early Church it seems to have been a part of the ceremony of baptism and some of the things that nowadays appear to be characteristic of confirmation are simply remnants of what used to belong to baptism as well. We think of confirmation as a particularly solemn public ceremony presided over by the bishop, but this was originally the case for baptism as well. Again, the special instruction nowadays associated with confirmation was at one time the normal accompaniment of baptism. We may come to understand confirmation better if we recall a strange phenomenon of the early Church. In apostolic times, baptism was frequently, even normally, accompanied by an outpouring of the Holy Spirit; the newly baptized began to prophesy, to "speak with tongues" and so on. For example when St. Paul came to Ephesus ". . . he met some disciples and said to them, 'Did you receive the Holy Spirit when you believed?' And they

said, 'No, we have never even heard that there is a Holy Spirit.'
And he said, 'Into what then were you baptized?' They said,
'Into John's baptism.' And Paul said, 'John baptized with the
baptism of repentance, telling the people to believe in the one
who was to come after him, that is, Jesus.' On hearing this
they were baptized in the name of the Lord Jesus. And when
Paul laid his hands upon them, the Holy Spirit came on them,
and they spoke with tongues and prophesied." [Acts 19.1–6.]

In the case of the household of the Gentile Cornelius, the
Holy Spirit came down even before they were baptized in sign
that they were to receive the sacrament:

> The believers from among the circumcized who came with
> Peter were amazed, because the gift of the Holy Spirit had
> been poured out even on the Gentiles. For they heard them
> speaking in tongues and extolling God. Then Peter declared,
> "Can anyone forbid water for baptizing these people who
> have received the Holy Spirit just as we have?" And he com-
> manded them to be baptized in the name of Jesus Christ.
> [Acts 10.45–8.]

Both these stories suggest that the outpouring of the Spirit
was normally regarded as a sort of confirmation of baptism,
and this may help us to understand the sacrament of confirmation. The Spirit comes on the baptized so that they prophesy
and bear witness to Christ. This, for both St. Luke and St.
John, is the essential work of the Spirit in the Church:

> You shall receive power when the Holy Spirit has come upon
> you; and you shall be my witnesses in Jerusalem and in all
> Judea and Samaria and to the end of the earth. [Acts 1.8.]
>
> When the Advocate comes, whom I shall send you from
> the Father, the Spirit of truth who proceeds from the Father,
> he will bear witness to me; and you also are witnesses,
> because you have been with me from the beginning. [John
> 15.26–7.]

The Holy Spirit, then, comes in confirmation so as to over-flow from him who receives it onto others, so that he becomes a source of the Spirit to others. We may compare the priest-hoods of baptism and confirmation to the two functions that we mentioned of the bishop; he offers sacrifice and he preaches. In each case what is done in a public official and sacramental way by the bishop is done in a personal way by the layman who is baptized and confirmed. The bishop exercises his priest-hood in offering the Mass by sacramental acts, the layman exercises his baptismal priesthood by his personal devotion. The bishop exercises his priesthood in witnessing to the Gospel by preaching, while the layman witnesses to it in more personal and complex ways.

It may be objected that there is no true parallel here, for while the bishop's priestly activity in offering the Mass is truly sacramental and is thereby distinguished from the exercise of baptismal priesthood, his work of preaching is not a sacramen-tal act and cannot thereby be distinguished from the witness of the layman.

It may be admitted that there is not an absolute parallel here, and yet many theologians today would hold that preach-ing, as a liturgical act, performed by the bishop or under his authority as a part of the Eucharist, is quasi-sacramental. That is to say its efficacy, like that of a sacrament, lies in an act of Christ and does not depend simply on the qualifications and skill of the preacher. The Spirit in the heart of the listener responds to the Spirit in the spoken word in a way that goes beyond the techniques of rhetoric. Exactly how this view is to be formulated without making preaching into an eighth sacra-ment is a question upon which theologians differ, and clearly it is a matter about which we have a good deal to learn from other Christian bodies who have always given preaching a central place in the Liturgy.

If these suggestions are true then we may say that in virtue of the priesthood of his confirmation a Christian has the power to witness to Christ, to bring the truth to his fellow men, in a way that goes beyond his skill in apologetics or the persuasiveness of his language; and this power will be exercised in function of his personal devotion to the truth and not, as with the priest or bishop, in function of an official liturgical role. The fact that holy men are especially effective in bringing to others an understanding of Christ cannot be explained simply in terms of "setting a good example". That the Doctors of the Church are theologians and saints indicates that theology itself is an exercise of the priesthood received at confirmation.

When St. Paul said to the men of Corinth, "My speech and my message were not in plausible words of wisdom, but in demonstration of the Spirit and power, that your faith might rest not in the wisdom of men but in the power of God" (1 Cor. 21.4–5), he was not necessarily referring to miracles he worked or even to the paranormal effects of the coming down of the Spirit; he may have meant simply the mysterious compelling force that the Spirit gave to his preaching. Christ's promise to the martyrs need not absolutely be confined to Christians in the courtroom:

> When they bring you before the synagogues and the rulers and the authorities, do not be anxious how or what you are to say; for the Holy Spirit will teach you in that very hour what you ought to say. [Luke 12.11–12.]

What I have said about confirmation is no more than a suggestion about where a theology of the sacrament might begin. There is a great deal more to be said. In particular, we should investigate the relation between the priestly authority associated with the episcopate and the analogous priestly authority associated with confirmation. This concerns authority in the family and in all kinds of education—also the interaction between the authority of the layman in these fields and that of the bishop.

One reason why confirmation has been so little studied in the past is that it is the sacrament of lay witness. It is only in modern times (apart, no doubt, from the very earliest years) that the laity has begun to play its proper part in the life of the Church. Of course there has been plenty of lay influence in the past, but this has commonly been the influence of politically powerful groups or individuals who have in one way or another found the Church useful for their purposes. Consciously or not, they have treated the Church as simply a stabilizing force in society, as inevitably on the side of the *status quo*. This has produced that alignment of the Church with parties of the Right and with the wealthy and privileged which is such a scandal to anyone familiar with the *Magnificat*. Those most concerned for the life of the Church have always been suspicious of this kind of lay influence. Today, however, we see something different. There has grown up an educated adult laity deeply concerned with the mission of the Church itself. The laity in many countries is shaking itself free of its proletarian condition and the consequences of this both for the organization of the Church and for its theology still remain to be worked out in full.

Even so brief an outline as this of the order of the Church would be incomplete without some reference to the diaconate. The story of its institution is well known:

> When the disciples were increasing in number, the Hellenists murmured against the Hebrews because their widows were neglected in the daily distribution. And the Twelve summoned the body of the disciples and said, "It is not right that we should give up preaching the word of God to serve tables. Therefore, brethren, pick out from among you seven men of good repute, full of the Spirit and wisdom, whom we shall appoint to this duty. But we will devote ourselves to prayer and the ministry of the word. [Acts 6.1–4.]

Seven were chosen and the Apostles "prayed and laid their hands upon them." It is clear that the deacons were instituted to take care of what we would now call the "temporalities" of the Church, the financial side of the parish or diocese. In token of this their liturgical function is to prepare the offerings of bread and wine for the Eucharist.

In the Western Church the order of the diaconate has for practical purposes disappeared. It is usually regarded as simply a step on the way to the priesthood, and in most places the deacon's work is done by priests. It is, however, becoming obvious that the business complications of a modern parish take up far too much of a priest's time and energy and involve him in the world of Mammon in a way inappropriate to his function. In some parishes, particularly in America, the finances of the parish have been handed over to a group of lay people with varying success. The obvious and traditional solution would seem to be a return to a real diaconate, an order of men devoted to the business side of the Church, having a definite part in the liturgical life of the parish and concerned, as deacons have traditionally been, with teaching as well as with finance. There would seem a very good case for dropping the rule of celibacy for such deacons.

Such a change would be a part of a general move towards levelling out the pyramid of authority in the Church. In the recent past the activity and authority of the Church has been, as it were, concentrated in a steep and tall hill surrounded by level country. This picture can represent both the concentration of authority in the Roman Curia vis-a-vis the bishops of the world, and the position of the parish priest vis-a-vis his parishioners. It would seem a better and more stable situation if there were a gently rising slope rather than a sudden precipice connecting the highest authorities in the Church and their subjects. In this way the priesthood of Christ would be shown forth in many different ways, sacramental and non-sacramental, amongst the members of his body.

Printed in the USA
CPSIA information can be obtained
at www.ICGtesting.com
LVHW011521070823
754510LV00003B/127